CREATING A
Positive School
Culture

How Principals and Teachers
Can Solve Problems Together

MARIE-NATHALIE BEAUDOIN
MAUREEN TAYLOR

Skyhorse Publishing

Skyhorse Publishing books may be purchased in bulk at special discounts for sales promotion, corporate gifts, fund-raising, or educational purposes. Special editions can also be created to specifications. For details, contact the Special Sales Department, Skyhorse Publishing, 307 West 36th Street, 11th Floor, New York, NY 10018 or info@skyhorsepublishing.com.

Skyhorse® and Skyhorse Publishing® are registered trademarks of Skyhorse Publishing, Inc.®, a Delaware corporation.

Visit our website at www.skyhorsepublishing.com.

10 9 8 7 6 5 4 3 2 1

Library of Congress Cataloging-in-Publication Data is available on file.

Cover design by Anthony Paular

Print ISBN: 978-1-63220-554-4
Ebook ISBN: 978-1-63220-971-9

Printed in the United States of America

CREATING A
Positive School
Culture

Contents

Preface

In the past decade, an increasing amount of pressure has been placed on school staffs to teach an expanding curriculum. At the same time, resources were decreased, responsibilities grew, and less time was made available for teachers to support each other.

As a result, issues often develop among staff members, such as negativity, isolation, or censure. This can cause principals and teachers to spend a tremendous amount of time and energy addressing these problems instead of focusing on academia, their initial goal. Educators and students alike may suffer.

Our intention in this book is to assist principals, with the collaboration of teachers, support staff, and parents, to form a school culture in which rich, supportive, and energizing relationships will be enhanced. Specifically, the purpose of this book is to help educators find efficient ways to understand and solve staff problems, prevent conflicts, and generally enrich their school culture. With that in mind, we gently invite readers to reflect on somewhat controversial questions and make visible the challenges of the current school system. Once visible, these challenges can be contained and practices can be developed to bring forth each person's wisdom and compassionate self. Narrative therapy, considered the cutting edge in systemic approaches, has been a very relevant theoretical framework to understand and address school culture issues. It offers a contextual perspective that fosters respect and awareness, and contributes to bringing the best out in everyone.

We have made every possible effort to write this book in a practical, clear, and creative way. Tutorials, exercises, common questions and answers, transcripts of conversations, illustrations, cartoons, dialogues between the authors, and numerous examples are used to keep the readers engaged with the material. This work is the result of many years of successful collaboration between a narrative therapist, consulting with several school principals, and a dedicated elementary school teacher. By combining therapeutic knowledge with day-to-day educational experience, the text provides a rich and comprehensive approach to a vast array of staff-related problems.

This book is *not* intended as an introduction to narrative therapy but rather as the application of narrative and social constructionist ideas to the field of education. For that reason narrative concepts are only covered in their relevance to teachers and principals, and the clinical practices associated with the ideas are not thoroughly examined. The interested reader can easily find further information on the subject in the many excellent introduction to narrative therapy books readily available (Bird, 2000; Freeman & Combs, 1996; Freeman, Epston, & Lobovits, 1997; Madsen, 1999; Winslade & Monk, 1999; White & Epston, 1990; Winslade & Monk, 2000; Zimmerman & Dickerson, 1996).

Embedded in the spirit of the narrative approach is the belief in local knowledges and in the wisdom of lived experience. Expertise is assumed to develop from the handling of everyday life and not simply from theoretical conceptualization. With that in mind, we could write a book marrying the narrative approach and education only by recruiting educators to share their experiences. We believe this has significantly enriched the material that we present and certainly inspired us greatly in the ideas that we propose. As a result, we have interviewed and/or surveyed well over 200 educators from a wide range of elementary and middle public schools in Northern California. The populations in these schools varied in terms of socioeconomic status, race, and ethnicity. Schools were visited in rural and suburban areas as well as in the city. Four schools involved parent participation, while the remaining were general public schools. The questionnaires, surveys, and interview format for this research are included in Resources D and E.

From those conversations we have extracted pressures, struggles, solutions, and reflections that color each individual's journey in schools. We have integrated all of the emerging themes into different sections. The first chapter of the book explores the experiences of principals and teachers in the subculture of the school system. Our intention in writing this section is to foster a greater understanding of people's struggles and experiences in schools, regardless of their respective roles. It covers in particular the pressures that constrain their ways of being and includes quotes from our research that reveal both the humor and hardship of the job. Chapter 2 presents a few fundamental principles and practices inspired by the narrative approach. A careful attempt has been made to eliminate most of the jargon embedded in the theory to render it accessible and relevant to educators. Chapter 3 details the climate problems that can emerge in systems under pressure such as schools. It covers, for example, the numerous problems presented to us by educators, such as gossip, cliques, and union conflicts, as well as more educational themes, such as competition, hierarchy, and evaluation. Chapter 4 offers a complete case analysis of the development of a climate problem and its solution. Chapter 5 engages the reader in the step-by-step process of inviting a group of staff members to change without triggering conflicts. Chapter 6 summarizes the ingredients of a strong school culture. Chapter 7 offers words of wisdom, ideas, suggestions, and strategies shared by principals to prevent or solve problems. Finally, Chapter 8 offers brief suggestions and perspectives for working with other adults in the school, such as parents and yard duty volunteers.

We hope that all readers will be inspired by at least one of the ideas exposed and will finish their reading energized to explore new possibilities with their colleagues. Above all, we hope that the book will bring forth more appreciation and compassion for yourself and the dedicated members of your community.

Acknowledgments

As in our first book of this project, *Breaking the Culture of Bullying and Disrespect, Grades K–8*, we would like to express our gratitude to all the educators who have participated in our research. In particular, we would like to acknowledge the staff from the following schools who have taken the time to kindly answer our lengthy surveys: Anderson School, Baker School, Country Lane School, Easterbrook School, Moreland Discovery School, and Rogers Middle School. Heartfelt acknowledgments are sent to those teachers from other schools across California who opened their classrooms to us: Sequoia Baioni, Maria Diaz-Albertini, Melissa Freeberg, Mariah Howe, Cathy Klein, Karen Lam, Kayla Meadows, Peter Murdock, Mary Robson, Sara Saldana, Chris Telles, the staff at Christa McAuliffe, Stuart Williams, and the staff at Cedarwood Sudbury School.

Interviews and e-mails with the following educators were also invaluable in that they provided a rich forum for personal stories and for in-depth accounts of their experiences in the education system. Given that some of these interviews were lengthy, often from one to two hours, we are eternally thankful for their trust, honesty, and generosity of time despite their busy schedules:

Les Adelson, Carolyn Barrett, Ann Dubois, Honey Berg, Martha Cirata, Nancy Cisler, Denise Clay, Carin Contreras, Harry Davis, Mindy Dirks, Bob Geddes, Maria Hansen-Kivijarvi, Faith Johnson, Tom Kennedy, Mary Anne Landis, Rick Ito, Sue Healy, Dale Jones, Debbie Judge, Barbara Lateer, Michele Mandarino, Heidi Meade, Bill Menkin, Alison Moser, Cleo Osborn, Joe Pacheco, Beverly Prinz, Herb Quon, Jim Richie, Lorie Rizzo, Kathleen Ryan, Louise Santos, Maria Simon, Bitsey Stark, Gary Stebbins, Mary Alice Tallahan, Stephany Tyson, Tiffany White, John Wise, and Jenny Wishnac.

We wish to thank the numerous other principals, teachers, and students who greatly contributed to this project and yet wish to remain anonymous.

Our gratitude goes daily to those creative, inspiring folks from the Bay Area Family Therapy Training Associates

(BAFTTA) who have kindly reviewed and edited the manuscript for narrative congruency as well as contributed to the statistical analysis:

Jeff Zimmerman, Ph.D.

Sonja Bogumill, Ph.D.

We are also indebted to the gracious individuals who have provided wisdom, support, and a variety of ideas during the length of this project:

Leisha Boek, Susan Brown, Kristi Busch, Fritz Dern, Erin Devinchenzi, Miles Gordon, Suzanne Hicklin, Krista Poston, Annie Prozan, Mari Rodin, Linda Rough, Sherry Stack, Judy Volta, May Walters, and Anne Woida.

We are grateful to the following professionals: Melanie Birdsall, our production editor, who was quite efficient and very refreshing to work with; Debbie Bruce, our cartoonist, who had a remarkable knack for creating delightful expressions of our ideas; and Rachel Livscy, our acquisitions editor, who was patient, skilled, and sincere.

Finally, last but not least, we offer great thanks and affection to the following generous, loving, and patient souls . . .

Amelia, Brian, David, Francine,
Jack, Jeff, Judy, Magnolia,
Marlene, Meika, and Paul.

The contributions of the following reviewers are gratefully acknowledged:

RoseAnne O'Brien Vojtek, Ph.D.
Principal
Ivy Drive Elementary School
Bristol, CT

Charles F. Adamchik, Jr.
Teacher/Educational Consultant
Blairsville High School and Learning Sciences International
Blairsville, PA

Gerald Monk
Professor
San Diego State University
San Diego, CA

John Winslade, Ph.D.
California State University, San Bernardino
San Bernardino, CA

About the Authors

Marie-Nathalie Beaudoin, Ph.D., is the training director at Bay Area Family Therapy Training Associates (BAFTTA) and supervises the counseling work in several schools in Silicon Valley, California. She has devoted much of her career to working with children, teaching tolerance projects, and improving staff relationships in public schools. Marie-Nathalie has been invited as a consultant to Bright House and Boston Consulting Group to assist them in improving the internal climate of an established Fortune 100 company. She is also an adjunct professor at John F. Kennedy University, where she teaches cross-cultural awareness, family therapies, and group dynamics. Marie-Nathalie has presented at numerous conferences and has published articles on narrative therapy, the *Silencing Critical Voices* journal (www.voices.com), and two other books, *Breaking the Culture of Bullying and Disrespect, Grades K–8*, and *Working With Groups to Enhance Relationships*.

Maureen Taylor is an educator in Northern California. Her background is in teaching preschool through sixth grade and being an environmental educator. Her main interests lie in teaching science and writing, two subjects that gently unfold for the learner. Maureen is currently developing a program for children blending art, environmental education, and social issues. She has coauthored *Breaking the Culture of Bullying and Disrespect, Grades K–8*, with Marie-Nathalie.

To all the educators of the world who commit their hearts and spirits to the blossoming of young minds

—MNB

With love to the Estherettes, Teapot Quincy y mi chunketue

—MT

CHAPTER ONE

Understanding the Different Experiences of Teachers and Principals

M ost educators can probably relate to the following three scenarios.

Everyone thinks of Karen as the Mother Teresa of the school. She is well known for going the extra mile, helping students at recess, bringing in items for needy families, and spending evenings in her classroom hosting parent gatherings. She attended the latest conferences on character education and positive discipline, and held a staff workshop to share the latest information from the conferences. Karen, however, feels like a fraud. She knows that she often yells at her students, and she feels guilty because she recognizes it reduces her classroom's morale. She finds herself yelling anyway.

Why does Karen yell, against her intentions and better judgment?

John enjoys his job as a principal. He likes to lead by example and makes great effort to visit classrooms daily. He has received many kudos for his dedication to his community. Recently, however, staff members have become upset by his absences during lunch. John has been going off campus more and more often to have lunch alone; for the staff, this means he is gone when they most need support and time to run ideas by him. Many perceive this act as a reflection of a deep lack of care, and question his reliability and authenticity.

Why does John "run away" despite the pleas of his staff?

Chris is the newest teacher on staff. He is well respected for having good control of his class and being enthusiastic about curriculum development. The mostly female staff appreciate having such a compassionate, masculine figure on site, especially one who is so kind and devoted to his work in education. To everyone's amazement, Chris is noticeably shy with the elderly woman who volunteers for lunchtime yard duty and seems to avoid her whenever possible. Some staff are beginning to question why Chris would act in this manner.

Why is Chris so distant with this woman, when he is so good with colleagues and children?

Why? Why? Why? is the question that many educators, principals and teachers alike, strive to answer when faced with an interpersonal challenge. There is a belief that we should understand the cause of a problem before we can even attempt to solve it: You can't fight an enemy you don't know. Yet many of the explanations we usually come up with focus on individuals, their believed personality, their "strengths" and "weaknesses."[1] In so doing, the personal and professional context of those people's lives is often forgotten. Often, the context of people's lives has at least an equal or greater influence on people's actions than any individual choice (see Beaudoin & Taylor, 2004, for more information). The context will determine if you are your outgoing and funny self or your more shy and reserved self. It is important to understand context because it:

1. Has the power to shape each individual's action

2. Colors how people expect others to behave

3. Is the backdrop against which problems develop

Consequently, no school culture can be truly addressed in any significant way until the context and the experiences of people are well understood. The more you know about the context and its unique impact on the individuals involved, the more power you have to address the situation effectively.

Whether you are a principal or a teacher, this chapter will:

- Assist you in articulating your own experience and depersonalize the struggles associated with your role
- Give you an insider's view into the responsibilities and pressures experienced by your colleagues
- Connect you further with compassion for others' responsibilities (compassion is always handy when addressing interpersonal tensions!)
- Allow you to use the ideas presented in the rest of the book successfully!

Principals often think they understand teachers' experiences because most of them "have been there"; in our research that has not proven to be true, as the leadership demands on principals often take precedence over remembering what it was like to be in a classroom. In addition, we tend to forget the nuances of experiences that have not been specifically named. For example, you may remember feeling generally overwhelmed at the end of the year but you may not (especially when overwhelmed) have actually articulated, named, and reflected upon exactly what happened. This makes it difficult to remember the details and implications of the experience. Finally, people's experiences on a principal career path can be distinct from those of other teachers in subtle ways. Your reference point provides only one perspective; certainly a valuable one, but it may overlap in limited ways with the integrated feedback of large numbers of educators.

This being said, let us now explore briefly the experience and work context of

a. Principals
b. Teachers

PRINCIPALS[2]

- What are the stories you have about who principals are as people?
- What comes to your mind when thinking "principals should . . ."?
- Which ones of these "shoulds" may be unrealistic?

These are some of the main questions we sought to understand as we interviewed a large number of administrators from a variety of districts and communities. What we found over and over again was that principals' daily lives were dominated by three experiences:

- Being mistaken for God
- Doing more, more, more
- Being everything for everyone all the time

Being Mistaken for God

People almost expect the principal to supply them everything they need, as if you were a counselor or a mommy or had a magic wand. I realized they wanted me to be God. I thought, "Oh, I didn't apply for that job. I think the position is already filled!"

—Elementary School Principal

What are the implications of being mistaken for God? When someone places you on a pedestal or overestimates your authority, you become trapped into a role where you cannot be your preferred self and must instead:

- Never make mistakes
- Know all the answers
- Be able to solve everything
- Control everything at will (parents, students, cafeteria issues, etc.)
- Predict the future (e.g., school enrollment or even the weather)

An elementary school principal spoke of this:

The teachers expect that you will never make a mistake. That is an unreasonable expectation. I once had a teacher say, "You called a rainy day lunch and it did not rain. You ruined my whole week!"

Principals are often assumed to have unlimited amounts of authority in controlling students, parents, teachers, circumstances, and the school environment. The pressure of being powerful takes on a life of its own, becoming a story. It is then repetitively confirmed by the noticing of only certain events over which the principal actually does have a certain power.

Those events are, in reality, of a limited nature. Upon closer analysis, three words distinguish a principal's actual power: narrow, solitary, and visible.

First, the power is narrow, limited in scope, and applied to only very specific issues. People experiencing a principal's power may experience it as intense, but on a broader scale of time and school culture it may have only a small effect. For example, a principal may have the choice to transfer or lay off a teacher, an action that has an intense effect for that teacher, but that same principal may be unable to affect a broader issue, such as changing a school's culture.

Second, the power is solitary, meaning that it is held by one individual in the face of a larger group of subordinates. Although it may seem as though the principal holds more power than a group of adults, regardless of the group's size and whether it is made up of teachers or parents, this solitary voice in reality can become very insignificant. We have spoken to many principals who wish they could implement a new practice, yet have been turned down by the majority. Ultimately there may be a popular and/or vocal teacher on staff who may hold more influential power over such items.

Third, the power is visible to all in the community. Because of the distinct nature of his or her role in the school, the principal is also the civic representative and the one to lead publicly. This visible power can lead to an inflated, unrealistic perception or story of the principal as a person and as a professional. Following are some comments from principals:

I was promoted to assistant principal, and soon teachers who had twenty or thirty years' experience were asking me for advice, though I felt they had been teaching much longer than I had.

—Middle School Assistant Principal

When you go from the classroom into that office, all of sudden people look at you different, as if you have been gifted with all the answers in education. Sometimes we feel like we should; they expect us to! They don't realize we are just human, just like them.

—Middle School Principal

Teachers feel they personally have limited amounts of power and know that the principal has somewhat more power, without knowing the limit of that power. The power is visible, yet the limit is often invisible.

Principals don't have a lot of power, and anyone going into a principalship for power is in for a rude awakening. If there is power, it's shared power. You're in between a rock and a hard place, meaning you have to keep the parents happy, the teachers happy and the district office happy. Sometimes these are at opposing places. I don't think I have power. I say "sorry" a lot and "what do you want me to do?" If you say to [people], "Is there something you want me to do?", many times they don't know, but they feel better that you listened to them.

—Elementary School Principal

There is a disconnection that may exist between teachers and principals in terms of understanding each other's realities. This is particularly true in regard to principals' lives, which may appear much more unpredictable and multifaceted to others than the known and visible routine of teachers. In other words, people get only a glimpse of a principal's day and may remain totally unaware of the full story. The pressure placed on principals to be powerful can have a whole set of undesirable consequences. This distorted story can, on one hand, create a context where teachers feel less capable than they actually are, engage in relationships in a disempowered way, and avoid responsibility on issues they could significantly affect. Teachers may end up taking a more passive role and expect principals to solve problems that pertain to everyone: "You have the power here . . . what are you going to do?"

As for principals, it can leave them with a false sense of entitlement and trying to impose demands on their staff (which typically backfires). Enormous amounts of responsibility can also bear heavily on one person's shoulders and create a context where mistakes are not only unavoidable but also accentuated by the community and difficult to forgive.

When teachers put you too high up it changes the way they treat you and ask questions. It puts the decision on you, which is bad because then you are responsible for everything. If you think someone is way up there, then you can't have honest conversations.

—Middle School Principal

Finally, the unrealistic story of principals as super powerful can create a false impression of them as invulnerable, without any particular human "needs" of their own and able to take in a lot of grief without being seriously affected.

Doing More, More, More

When the school year starts in August, you hit the ground running and you never stop. The school year is one big sprint.

—Middle School Principal

In most school districts, principals are responsible for: planning student assessments, class placement, discipline, student study teams, clubs, sports, yard duty, lunch duty, administrative paperwork, observations, district meetings, planning, staff development, staff evaluation, grants, leading staff meetings, spreading information, memo writing, facilities, traffic, buses, cafeteria, food delivery, parents, Home and School Club, homework center meetings, community programs, counselor, planning assemblies, grade-level meetings, coordinating prep times, evaluate absentee rates, test scores, research, fundraising, supervising, conferencing, teaching, modeling, coordinating parent help, hiring process, firing process, conferences, professional growth, accommodating visitors, emergency contact, financial work/budget, staff cheerleader . . . and so on.

This pressure places an enormous amount of responsibilities on principals and can be unrealistic. Over the past hundred years, schools have been increasingly institutionalized and have faced more complex sets of requirements. The educational system has been facing more demands while being burdened with a limited budget. As a result the government has simply resorted to increasing the principal's workload. Given that, in many states, administrators do not have the luxury of an organized union's protection, they often feel forced to subject themselves to those demands with little possibility of protest. As discussed by two California principals:

If you don't know how to work with the superintendent, you're out. [In my area] there is no union to back you up. You work at the pleasure of the superintendent.

—Middle School Principal

A teacher once asked me when I was going to get tenure! I told her that [here] we don't get tenure. We don't even have a year-to-year contract. Our work is day to day. You simply have to do the best job you can for your people.

—Middle School Principal

In other words, if educators are really committed to the work of leadership, their only real option is to do so with all the additional tasks. This can remind us of the situation a century ago, when employers subjected workers without job security to excessive amounts of work. The biggest difference in this situation is that there is practically no one to replace principals if they decide to leave.

How far can this go? How many more demands can be placed on principals? Current data reveal there may soon be a principal shortage, as people are less willing to work an average of 54 hours a week, in stressful conditions, with lack of resources, increasing responsibilities, and a sense that the compensation, in certain districts, can result in a pay cut when actual hours of work are factored in (Education Writers Association, 2002). In the meantime, current principals have the sense that they never can do enough.

Such a high level of accountability, to many different groups with different goals and preferences, also means that you can never satisfy everyone; you always receive some criticism and very little appreciation.

Having to let go a teacher, for example, is very difficult. If you keep the person, the staff may be upset because you are keeping a bad apple; if you ask them to leave, those who have bonded with the teacher will be upset. And then you have to live with this situation 'till the end of the year.

—Elementary School Principal

Our middle school team has worked hard with the union to organize a late-morning start on Wednesdays so that teachers can meet and collaborate with each other. We were very pleased to make that possible for teachers, and it is certainly in the best interest of students. Parents, however, started calling and were upset thinking that their children might miss out on academics. We really can never satisfy everyone.

—Middle School Principal

Other effects of this pressure may be: exhaustion, imbalance of personal and professional life, feeling overwhelmed, and depression.

I know it will never be enough even if I stay here every night until 10. It has tremendous effect on family life. Sometimes I don't see my children for several days, and, even when I am sitting home on a Sunday thinking "it's me time," I'm not able to be present. My mind is still at school.

—Middle School Principal

Finally this pressure demands such an extreme amount of work focused on the community's children and families that, ironically, very little time can be left for one's own. It is not surprising that the turnover rate for principals between 1988 and 1998 was 42% and that approximately 40% of principals leave the field because of politics, bureaucracy, and unreasonable demands (Education Writers Association, 2002).

Being Everything for Everyone All the Time

The principal is often perceived as the person to go to if you have a problem, particularly if it is a big problem. People are aware of their own needs and do not necessarily realize that their demands are multiplied by at least 30 other staff and countless families. We have heard teachers and parents wonder what a principal does with his or her time, especially if the principal does not respond that very day to a question or request.

We once met with a principal at 1 P.M. We walked in as she was just finishing checking her e-mail. She announced to us that while she was busy on lunch duty, the district office had sent an e-mail, expecting all administrative staff to meet at the district office at 1 P.M. We stood there, stunned that a district could possibly mandate principals to be at a meeting an hour and a half after an e-mail had been sent.

Principals clearly experience a pressure to be available. Principals have to be willing to drop everything and do what the district prioritizes for them. They have to be at the beck and call of the system and able to meet many multiple demands. Principals have to ensure that everyone is happy, the school is running smoothly, and all the paperwork is completed.

The implications of this pressure are great. First, principals can never fully know in the morning how their day will go—will they have to be prepared for a life-threatening emergency or have a peaceful day? They have to be somewhat on guard all the time and can never totally relax or achieve a sense of control over their day.

My biggest "Aha!" when I went from a being a teacher to being a principal was that I can never control my day. As a teacher, I would spend hours planning for every hour of every day. However, as a principal, I could have nothing on my planner for a particular day and that day will end up being crazy!

—Elementary School Principal

Second, such bombardments of requests by many people require that decisions be made quickly. This may result in decisions that are not always ideal and may not even represent what the principals themselves would have preferred, given a chance to reflect, as illustrated in the following comments:

You have to make these quick decisions and then later on you realize . . . Oh . . . no . . . did I really say that?

—Elementary School Principal

At school you have to make so many decisions so quickly that you end up not being as collaborative as you'd like. Things come back from your staff to bite you if you make too many decisions in isolation.

—Elementary School Principal

Third, principals not only have to be everything for everyone all the time at school, but this pressure carries into their personal lives. Specifically, numerous principals have shared how any public appearance has the possibility of turning into a school conversation, whether they want it to or not. This is particularly true of principals living in or near the community served by their school.

In many ways, this pressure does not allow principals the freedom to perform other identities in their public community, or the space to enjoy the richness of their lives and the multiple roles they wish to fulfill.

> *I live in this community. It's 24–7. When I go out, for example to a softball game, all the parents approach me and want to talk about their kids. I don't mind sometimes, but sometimes I'm with my godchildren or I'm coaching, and I don't get to just be a person. My principal friend and I laugh because you never go out in shorts and sandals with messy hair. I can't be seen buying beer. You feel like you have to explain that you really still are a good role model.*
>
> —Elementary School Principal

> *It would be nicer if more people got that I'm a person, I'm not just the administrator. There is a tendency on the part of people to think that the administrator is a different animal. I am a parent, I am a human being, I am a mother, I am a wife, I am a runner, I'm a lot of things. What I do here is another skill that I have, and I'm a person underneath it all.*
>
> —Elementary School Principal

In Sum . . .

These three pressures (being mistaken for God; doing more, more, more; and being everything for everyone all the time) have the effect of rendering a principal's life highly stressful, can create a sense of inadequacy in the face of unrealistic demands, can be isolating, and may lead to burnout. We were inspired by a middle school principal's description of the experience of this role (Figure 1.1): "A principal has to walk this difficult obstacle course with a beach blanket Babylon hat, with everything attached on it— school safety, scores, budget, buses, traffic, cafeteria, etc. They have to keep everything balanced while everybody is watching you, evaluating how you're solving problems, and wondering if you're going to fall into crocodile-infested waters."

Figure 1.1   Principals have to keep everything balanced while they walk an obstacle course and are evaluated for their performance

As will be discussed later in this book, many principals remain in the profession for their commitment to children and find ways to deal with these pressures. As illustrated in the following box, humor keeps many of them going!

Box 1.1   Creative Metaphors About the Role of Principal

- "When you are the principal, sometimes you"re the bug, sometimes you're the windshield!"
- "A principal has to keep on swimming upstream, despite the current, the storms, and the dams."
- "Being a principal is like being a sewing machine, stitching things together and joining the different fabrics."
- "Being a principal sometimes feels like acting in a Shakespearean play . . . you can't leave during one of the tragic parts, only when the play is completed."
- "Being a principal is like operating a TV remote control. If used unconsciously, one can get trapped into spinning through all the choices that are available and never focusing on one important thing. If used for its intent (to be more efficient), it can be seen as a way to maneuver through a lot of information and make a choice that saves time and brings a focus to time spent."
- "Principals can act as manure or fertilizer. The potential is there for them to do things that stink a lot, but you can also very much help things grow."
- "A principal is like a Cuisinart. It does all the different tasks with the different attachments. It takes different ingredients, mixes them all together, and makes a new product. It's really fast, so you are dizzy all the time."
- "When you are a principal, you act as a watering can. You fill it up and nurture everyone to grow: parents, teachers, and kids. One seed won't grow alone and you have to give them all water. You also have to find out how to fill up your watering can."

- "Being a principal is like being a mom . . . you are everything to everybody. You are always reminding people to do things and console them when they are hurt. You are trying to please everybody but you can't."
- "Being principal is like being Don Quixote. In the face of all the obstacles, you just stay hopeful, believe in your people, and believe that the best is possible."
- "A principal is like an underwater juggler. You hold your breath, hoping everything goes where it is supposed to, but everything floats away. Sometimes you come up for air, see land, and things are the way you thought they would be. So you think, 'Oh, I'll just go back on down; it's all right.'"
- "Being a principal is like being a car going down the highway ninety miles an hour."
- "Being a principal is like being Jiminy Cricket. You are always showing up at the right times saying all the right things to keep them going."
- "A principal is like a butterfly . . . people do mistake you for a Godlike creature but you are simply fluttering around campus, hoping to help someone have a better day and doing your best to make people's lives more productive."

TEACHERS

As most groups in any given culture, teachers receive pressure to be a certain way. These standards are often unspoken and are assumed to come naturally with the profession. It is interesting to explore how these pressures evolve over time and how they differ or continue. Here is an amusing look at published rules for teachers at the beginning of the 20th century.

Rules for Teachers—1915

1. You will not marry during the term of your contract.

2. You are not to keep company with men.

3. You must be home between the hours of 8 P.M. and 6 A.M. unless attending a school function.

4. You may not loiter downtown at ice cream shops.

5. You may not travel outside the city limits unless you have permission of the chairman of the board.

6. You may not ride in a carriage or an automobile with any man unless he is your father or brother.

7. You may not smoke cigars.

8. You may not wear bright colors.

9. You may under no circumstances dye your hair.

10. You must wear at least two petticoats.

11. Your dresses must not be any shorter than 2 inches above the ankles.

12. To keep the schoolroom neat and clean, you must sweep the floor at least once daily, scrub the floor at least once a week with hot soapy water, clean the blackboard at least once a day, and start the fire at 7 A.M. so the room will be warm by 8 A.M.

SOURCE: Cabell County West Virginia Board of Education, Old Sacramento Schoolhouse Museum.

- Which one of these pressures still exists for teachers in the 21st century?
- If you were to write the rules for the present time, what would come to mind?
- Do you find current pressures to be very different from the rules published in 1915?
- What are the effects of these pressures on teachers' job satisfaction, relations with each other, and performance as educators?

Intrigued by these questions, we surveyed and/or interviewed 240 teachers from a variety of public schools in California. These teachers have various degrees of experience and work in school districts with a wide range of population, ideologies, and socioeconomic status.[3]

In our research most teachers reported that the pressures to be a certain way were very strong (4 or 5 on a scale of 1 to 5). Four main pressures were identified as placing significant stress on teachers. The pressures were to (1) sacrifice personal time; (2) be super responsible; (3) always be in control; and (4) be perfect role models. As such, the current rules for teachers at the turn of the 21st century could be playfully written as follows:

Rules for Teachers—2004

1. You will do constant "little" extras
2. You will embody responsibility and be "on," always
3. You will never smile before Christmas
4. You will be 100% pure and conservative

While reading this section, some readers will relate more than others to certain pressures. These reactions can be based on their personal experience of race, class, gender, subculture of current school, and various other life occurrences. Also, pressures may vary in how they are expressed from one school environment to another. Let us now explore each one of these pressures in more detail.

You Will Do Constant "Little" Extras

Most teachers are hard-working professionals and feel the pressure to work long hours. Society expects teachers to sacrifice and overwork in the name of dedication. In many schools there is a pressure, an unspoken message, that working long hours and doing "little" extras proves your commitment to students. While dedication in itself is a beautiful way of being, the problem lies in that there is no limit to the amount of work that needs to be done. The possibility of dedication becomes unlimited. You could always:

Create a new lesson

Clean your classroom

Change decorations in your classroom

Write more anecdotal records on your students

Write another parent newsletter

Plan another field trip

Surf the Internet for resources

Head up a new committee

Answer e-mail messages from parents

Call a parent

Write more feedback on papers

Learn something new

Support a new teacher

Develop new curriculum

Take an online course

Mentor a student

Collaborate with a colleague

Add to this list

In our survey, systematically all teachers, when asked directly, reported having to sacrifice personal time to get the job done, and 83% of those teachers said they sacrificed personal time to complete their job most of the time or always. As stated by one teacher,

> *You could work as many hours as you want. You would never find an end to your time. Even when I go places and do activities with my family, I see [everything] as a teacher. I'm always thinking, "What can I use? This would be neat."*

—Fifth Grade Teacher

Teachers are expected not only to teach their curriculum but also to tend to the extra needs of families and students, often during personal time. Teachers who work at a school with financially privileged families shared with us that a great deal of pressure was based around constantly providing more academic curriculum for students. This requires the preparation of challenging academic exercises and a richer curriculum. Other teachers find themselves working long hours focused on after-school activities and clubs, mentoring, tutoring, and socially caring for underprivileged neighborhood children.

Again, while a certain amount of dedication and little extras in one's work are not bad in themselves, in excess they have two major implications. They imply that teachers are pushed into sacrificing some of their personal time for their work. This may be a painful dilemma, costly both to family relationships and well-needed self-care activities. As illustrated by the following teacher comment:

Sometimes I feel so rushed and so tired and I think I come to school looking tired and drained. I feel like some parents want me to be perfect and perky with nylons and dressed to a T. I can't do that when I stay up until 11 grading and get here early in the morning to do something. I am so tired and I have no time for me. I look like I got hit. I can't go work out; I have to get this done. I find I don't have that balance for the gym and eating right. I am a better teacher when I do that. I'm nicer. I have more patience.

—Fifth Grade Teacher

Box 1.2   In Their Own Words

Teachers Speak of the Pressures of Dedication and Sacrifice

- "Give 100% of your time to your class."
- "Keep a cute and immaculately clean classroom."
- "Accept the fact and do not complain about how little salaries are, and apologize for having summers off."
- "Pay for all cool classroom materials and buy things for your students."
- "Do not complain: teaching is an 'easy' job."
- "Don't take personal days off because the kids are depending on you, and there's a shortage of subs."
- "Provide students with tons of homework at levels above grade level."
- "Do all the necessary paperwork all the time and have exciting lessons planned for your students so that all students are busy all the time."
- "Solve *all* student learning and behavior problems."

Third, problems can develop when teachers chose not to fulfill the pressure of sacrifice and feel stigmatized by that difference. In the eyes of their school community, these teachers may be perceived as underperforming or less committed to the profession, even though they actually are, just not in that particular way. Teachers who are parents cannot win. If they put teaching above parenting, they may be questioned as a neglectful parent. If they put their family above teaching, they are in danger of not appearing as professional as others appear.

I had a difficult time balancing career and my son, mostly because of my feelings of hypocrisy. I felt that I was always trying to implement "best practice" for kids and then wasn't able to apply the same principles for my own. I felt that leaving him all day at the day care center was too long, and when I expressed wanting to leave our staff meeting early, it was met with strong objection. My principal told me that others resented it and said that we all had commitments (kids, appointments, personal lives) and I shouldn't be allowed to leave early if no on else could. I found this colored my outlook, and I scrutinized all demands on my time. I became really frustrated when we would be discussing, at length, a situation that was only applicable to one or two people (e.g., I can't get my e-mail to work. What do we serve for the brunch?). I think that my feelings were interpreted by others. They thought I was not caring enough for my students and school, that I was putting my child first and really didn't have a vested interest in that staff. I have never felt that the amount of time a teacher is at school (e.g., until 7 P.M. and on the weekends) is a just indicator of how effective or dedicated they are.

—Third Grade Teacher

In sum, the pressure of doing too many "little" extras and overly sacrificing personal time can have negative effects on individuals, school culture, and students. Common effects of this pressure on teachers include:

- Sacrificing their own needs for health, family, and personal space, which can eventually lead to dissatisfaction in their lives, family conflicts, and resentment against giving so much and not necessarily receiving significant appreciation in return
- Being drained of energy and, in some situations, facing professional burnout
- Feeling guilt and frustration. Teachers commonly worry that there is never enough time and that what is done is never enough or as much as one would like to do
- Doubting yourself and questioning your worth as an educator when you do set limits or try to be dedicated in ways that are different from those privileged by the pressure

Ironically, this pressure can also have negative effects on the teacher-student relationship. Although it may seem that students would gain from an overly dedicated teacher, it is questionable whether they gain on a level that is meaningful for them. Students may become more attached to and perform better for a teacher who is present, relaxed, and energetic than for a tired teacher who has prepared extra assignments. Teachers who spend enormous amounts of time and energy preparing as much as they can may sometimes become resentful of the lack of recognition and appreciation they get in return from students, principals, or colleagues.

In terms of the effects on the school culture, over-dedication can lead to comparison and competition as to who is the most dedicated and to a lack of time for bonding or supporting each other's work.

You Will Embody Responsibility and Be "On," Always . . .

Most people value the ability to be responsible. Having responsible staff members is necessary for schools to operate and is completely understandable in the context of the safety

> **Box 1.3**   In Their Own Words
>
> ### Teachers Speak of the Pressures to Be Responsible at All Costs
>
> - "Serve on numerous committees"
> - "Have *all* students at grade level by the end of the year"
> - "Cover *all* of the numerous state standards"
> - "Have neat, well-organized classrooms"
> - "Always keep in contact with all parents"
> - "Have their students score high on standardized tests"
> - "Teach math and language arts only: no art or 'frills'"
> - "Provide homework that is clearly explained to kids (for the ease of parents) to 'keep kids busy at home' and be responsible for its completion'

and education of large numbers of children. Being a responsible teacher usually implies being reliable, organized, and well prepared. These skills contribute to the survival of teachers, given the extreme and varied tasks that need to be accomplished. Teachers who are organized and responsible are often admired, consulted, and perceived as competent. Often, however, these teachers take on a lion's share of the work, and this can also have negative effects. Again, it is the excessive form of this pressure that causes problems, not its appropriate and necessary form. In our research, 82% of teachers reported feeling the pressure to be organized and well prepared (beyond their preference) most of the time. In other words, while most teachers clearly value these ways of being and choose to function in a responsible and organized way, there are frequent instances where they feel compelled to engage in behaviors that they personally don't value but that seem necessary to avoid stigmatization from the community. We would like you, the reader, to reflect for a brief moment on your own ways of being responsible and organized.

- What does being responsible mean to you?
- Are you responsible and organized to your satisfaction?
- Do others perceive you being as responsible and organized as you think you are?
- What if your ideas of responsibility don't fit those of your school colleagues and administrators?
- What if you want to be responsible in a different way?

Consider this story:

I consider myself a good teacher and one who takes her responsibility seriously. I worked in this school district for nearly 10 years and was only absent in extreme cases. I had to be really ill to call in sick. I felt irresponsible being away from my class. I knew I had a problem when a family member decided to host a family reunion out of my town, and it happened to be during the middle of the school year. Attending the reunion would mean that I would be absent from teaching my class for almost a week. My family is quite important to me and knowing this event would only come around every 10 years made me quite interested to go. I wanted to be with my family and, yet, the stress of missing school was eating me up. My plan was to be honest with my district, explain the importance of this family time, ensure that I found myself an experienced, reliable substitute teacher, and leave a detailed education plan for him or her. I thought this was quite responsible. After talking to some colleagues, I was confused because each one warned me against being honest with our administration. I decided to see what the teachers' union president would say. The advice I received was to call in sick, plain and simple. Don't tell anyone where you are going and hope that you don't run into anyone at the airport. Now I was in a bind. I had planned to be honest. I was now burdened with worries and angry that I was being compelled to lie. What if someone commented on my tan? What if I found something educational from my travels that I wanted to share with my class? What if I ran into someone at the airport? What if someone from school phoned my home and I wasn't there lying sick on the couch?

—Second Grade Teacher

If you were this teacher, what would you have done?

This story illustrates well how pressures in the school system narrow possibilities and force teachers to act against their own integrity and will. In this story, everyone lost because of narrow ideas about being responsible.[4]

The school would have been more able to responsibly find an appropriate substitute who would have benefited from the detailed education plan prepared by the teacher, which would have been more relevant and appropriate for the students, who could also have shared the excitement of their teacher's trip. When criteria for responsibility are too narrow and inflexible, problems arise. When teachers are expected to model predictability and reliability as workers beyond the normal variations of life circumstances, more problematic, rigid ways of being become promoted.

You Will Never Smile Until Christmas

"Education 101" stipulates that control of your class, especially early in the school year, is critical to establish the foundation of a successful, effective instructional year. Most teachers fear that not following this pressure would either promote some sort of chaos or would be judged severely by their peers. This was evident in our research, as 68% of teachers (when asked directly) reported the need to control their students *beyond their personal preference* at least half the time. Above all of the fears associated with student behaviors was the concern that an observer would visit and evaluate, negatively, the state of the class.

Box 1.4   In Their Own Words

Teachers Speak of the Pressures to Be in Control

- "Be strict and teach discipline"
- "Be in tight control of the class"
- "Keep classes silent when working, so you have a quiet 'you-could-hear-a-pin-drop' classroom"
- "Always be responsible for behavior of students"
- "Stay on top of them, don't let them get out of hand for a second"

- What is your personal definition of being in control of your class?
- What percentage of the time do you control your class to your satisfaction?
- Would your principal and colleagues agree with that number, or would they have a different estimate?

Although a certain amount of control can definitely be useful and necessary in some instances, an excessive focus on this issue can actually be costly to teachers and have the opposite effect. For example, the expectation of control can get teachers to spend a large amount of energy worrying and plotting new ways to use classroom management ideas. It can also influence them to be strict and impatient—not their preferred self. It can create an unrealistic context where one person (granted, an adult) is expected to be responsible for the behavior of thirty others. In its extreme form, this pressure, more than any other, can drain teachers' energy and enthusiasm. Some teachers even report feeling trapped between either connecting with their colleagues and being distant with students or connected with students but being distant from their colleagues. The following two stories illustrate these experiences, the first one being from a rather petite teacher who chose to be connected with her students while the second story illustrates a teacher's painful dilemma in attempting to stay connected with a colleague.

In the early 70s, I was teaching big classes and had found that the students worked best in small groups. These classes fairly bubbled with energy, and it sometimes happened that the door of the classroom was suddenly thrown open by the principal or vice-principal, who would stand with hands on hips and roar, "When your teacher is not in the classroom, I don't want to hear a sound out of you!" At such times I could never decide if it was worse to stand up and reveal that I was in fact present, or just to wait until he finished glaring and left! Whenever I tried later to explain my methods and reasons to the administration, there was no respect for such innovation, only respect for silence in the classroom. Years later I met one of my former students by accident, and she was very happy to see me again. She thanked me for these classes, as she had never forgotten the unique humanness of that environment in the midst of the rigidity of the school's style of education.

—Second Grade Teacher

Many years ago, I decided to share a classroom because I needed time to take care of educational demands and family needs. I was paired with a teacher who was thoughtful and passionate about teaching. We had things in common, so we assumed our management styles would be similar. As it turned out, she was more structured and controlling than I, and also more outspoken about her management program. I agreed to try to use it since I knew we should be consistent. My awkwardness grew as time went on because I knew I didn't want to control kids so much; I was used to a more democratic approach. The thing I most noticed was that my relationship with the kids was distant, like never before in my years of teaching. I attributed it to my not being there full time, yet later when I thought about it more, I realized it was because I was uncomfortable laying down thick laws, a strict point system, and not resolving conflicts in a way I was used to.

—Third Grade Teacher

Ironically, teachers themselves do not even meet those expectations. . . . Think back to those staff meetings. Consider those staff members who whisper their opinions to their neighbors, giggle in the back of the room, correct papers while the meeting is going on, allow their cell phones to interrupt, and make unmannerly comments during discussions.

When control is the overriding theme, the school culture also suffers. The pressure to control in some schools is so high that the level of excitement for learning barely exists. Such pressure creates a stressful environment for both teachers and students, who may experience disconnection and disengagement.

You Will Be 100% Pure

There clearly is a professional pressure that requires teachers to be good role models. Most of the time, this pressure matches with teachers' intentions, since they willingly want to help children understand the socially agreed-upon "acceptable" behaviors. Schools were created to assist children in becoming "good citizens." Problems arise from the limited ways in which a good role model or good citizen is defined— what it includes and what it excludes. In other words, the issue lies in the narrow criteria dictated by the pressure and its invasiveness in all areas of life.

Half of all teachers responding to the open-ended survey reported experiencing the pressure to be a good role model, and, when asked directly, 90% of teachers reported feeling the good-role-model pressure most of the time.

Being a good role model often means replicating and modeling the political beliefs and values of the dominant

Box 1.5   In Their Own Words

**Teachers Speak of the Pressure
to be a Good Role Model**

- "Reflect present political views, and be conservative"
- "Always smile; be happy, patient and agreeable"
- "Never get mad"
- "Be nurturing"
- "Always be professional and prompt"
- "Radiate confidence and remain positive"
- "Get along with everyone"
- "Behave with a higher standard of behavior outside of the classroom than other people (even higher than parents)"
- "Do not drink alcohol or smoke"
- "Always be well rested ('you work only nine months a year and only from 8:30 to 3')"
- "Have an impeccable memory (know 'Johnny's' name 10 years later)"
- "Of course, have perfect kids yourself"

culture—meaning white, middle class, heterosexual, and conservative. In our surveys, many teachers even reported the pressure to dress a certain way:

- "Dress in demure, modest, and conservative clothing"
- "Do not dye your hair, have body piercings or tattoos"
- "I can never run with my dog wearing old sweats"

The pressure around being a good role model requires that teachers walk, talk, and breathe according to society's standards of "acceptable" behavior. Many teachers have commented on the fact that they can never act totally free outside of their homes (unless the home is at a great distance from school). This pressure requires not only that teachers represent the dominant culture politically, but also that their actions are based in high moral standards. This means being a perfectly moral individual at all times, not only while at work. Even when the children are gone, anyone can walk into a teacher's classroom and make a judgment upon the appropriateness of her dress, her body language, her activities, and the cleanliness of her classroom, among other factors. When she leaves the school, a teacher is often conscious of the possible judgment or interpretation any bystander could make about everything. Within minutes, she could be judged on the vehicle she drives, the appearance of the car, any bumper stickers she has displayed, which type of music is coming from the car, where she is going, and if she is speeding.

This is even true when a teacher is enjoying a weekend or a holiday, as illustrated by the following story:

Once I was at the park on a weekend, enjoying a beer with lunch. I had on shorts and a bikini top because it was hot. As I played Frisbee, I heard, "Hi, Ms. M!" It was a student and his family. I felt completely awkward, as if I had been caught working at a strip club or something.

—Fourth Grade Teacher

As a result of this pressure, most teachers report hiding at least one aspect of themselves. In our surveys, 30% to 40% of teachers reported withholding personal information on a variety of items from their school colleagues. Aspects that were most commonly not disclosed fell in the categories of "experimentation during teen and college years" and "alcohol and drug use." Sexual orientation was the third most taboo subject, with close to 25% of teachers reporting that it was unsafe to share. These data are much higher than the proportion of gay, lesbian, and bisexual people in the general population, which is estimated at 10%. Overall, this shows that teachers are most likely to refrain from disclosing any personal information, especially if there is any risk of it being considered outside of dominant norms.

Question for Educators: What would *you* feel uncomfortable disclosing at your school site?

Why? _____

_____

For some of you, the discomfort would be so great that you may not even risk writing the information down in this book. For others, what you may or may not wish to disclose is not apparent to you, because you are used to functioning in such a way. Yet again, a few of you may have the good fortune of being at a school site where you have great trust and connection with your colleagues.

What are the effects of this pressure and the scrutiny associated with it? Teachers have to be aware that somewhere, somehow, someone could see them engage in socially questionable behaviors. The costs of having to follow this pressure, which may not fit for them, and also of being the subject of social scrutiny, can be great. Common effects of this situation include:

• *Isolation:* Especially if you have to hide an important part of yourself or your life. Examples of this include teachers from a different ethnicity, religion, or class or those struggling with an illness, a divorce, an out-of-wedlock pregnancy, political views, or simply hobbies that may stand outside of the norm. This isolation can disconnect these teachers from the rest of the staff and from their students, as they cannot fully relate. In other words, their whole sense of self cannot be involved genuinely in relationship.

• *Self-alienation:* Feeling like a fraud, like someone you are pretending to be

• *Wasted energy:* Spending energy engaging in practices that you don't necessarily believe in and filtering out your natural inclinations

• *Resentment and frustration:* Being sour about having to participate in this situation

In some ways, this pressure leads to expectations of teachers being icons of virtue in society. Given that teachers can never be a perfect role model, it may at times contribute to disrespect from the community. Parents may judge a teacher as being too strict or not strict enough, too nurturing or too cold, too academically focused or not focused enough . . . who can fit the narrow mold of the perfect role model?!

In some ways, teachers are "on" all the time. Regardless of location or time, they are seen as teachers. Whether the student-teacher relationship is current or not, the teacher will always be seen as a teacher. In other words, once a teacher, always a teacher. What are the effects of this good role model pressure on teachers' relationship with students? When a teacher develops contrived ways of dealing with students, potentially useful options of relating are left out along with the teacher's unique and creative talents. In addition, the narrow way of relating may not fit with all students' needs and leave some alienated, not to mention that all kids miss out on the possibilities of being exposed to the richness of each teacher's multiple ways of being.

In sum, the extreme pressure to be a perfect role model can have several negative effects on children by:

- Modeling limited ways of being
- Exposing children to only the dominant culture and leaving them less able to appreciate the value of diversity
- Depriving students who may not fit in the dominant culture of a valuable role model
- Confirming the necessity of pretending to be someone you are not, or of attempting to belong to the majority instead of accepting and honoring your differences

The expectation of high morality is more prevalent from adults than students, who in general connect more readily to a teacher's authentic self.

What are the effects of this pressure on the school culture? In extreme situations, the pressure on teachers to be perfect role models can create a false environment where everyone is pretending to be an icon of social perfection. In most situations, unfortunately, the staff know very little about each other as people, and, as a result, their conversation focuses on problem-saturated accounts of students or superficial conversations about work.

Conclusion

Which one of these pressures do you think would be amusing for people to read a century from now?

Although pressures can provide a sense of direction, their rigidity does not take into account the dynamics and complexity of relationships and context. As a result, these pressures can limit a teacher's access to possible solutions when faced with a challenging circumstance. These pressures

Figure 1.2   A teacher's mind and best judgment can become cluttered and impeded with confusing and opposing thoughts

can leave a teacher constantly doubting herself and her choices, which in the end can be very draining of energy and can actually contribute further to problems. This also contributes to the enormous teacher drop-out rate of 30% in the first five years (Merrow, 2001). In the end, a teacher's mind and best judgment can become cluttered and impeded with confusing and opposing thoughts. See Figure 1.2.

Despite all of these challenges, numerous individuals remain in education because of their love for children and the meaningful rewards of teaching (see the playful descriptions in the box below). In many ways this shows that these

---

Box 1.6   In Their Own Words

Teachers' Descriptions of Their Work Experience

- "Teaching is like a wild and crazy rafting adventure in mega challenging terrain . . . exhilarating, exciting, strenuous, exhausting, rewarding, and unpredictable, very up and down. One minute you are laughing and smiling, the next crying. But it's a rafting adventure for the huge cause of making a difference in the lives of others."
- "To be a teacher, you need to be able to have your eyes open, ears open, arms open, mind open, and heart open all the time."
- "Teaching is like being a Swiss Army knife, because you have to be ready each day and open to what tool is needed."
- "Teaching is quite a job! You are in charge of your own good time!"
- "Teaching children is like building a beautiful house . . . many tools are used, materials are needed, time is invested, and it is a labor of love."
- "Teaching is like holding the future in my hands."

(Continued)

Box 1.6 (Continued)

- "As a teacher, I have to be a symphony conductor. Sometimes the brass is too brash and the percussion is too loud. I sense the tempo and mood and alter it, if necessary."
- "Teaching can be a mini-adventure, almost every day."
- "Teaching is a box of chocolates. Each day is a surprise. You never know what you are going to get."

pressures can be minimized to a point where many people can have a satisfying work life and function at their best. An awareness of teachers' experiences of the context can foster not only greater compassion in the face of problems but also allow a more realistic and effective approach to the prevention and solving of complex problems.

NOTES

1. The concepts of personalities, strengths and weaknesses are introduced here as a reflection of the everyday conversations in schools. They are however incongruent with the post-structuralist philosophy presented in this book where individuals are not assumed to have a core personality with a set reservoir of assets/deficits but rather are constituted by multiple selves shaped by a variety of relationships and contexts. This will be explained further in a later section of this chapter.

2. Please note that by "principals" we mean both principals and assistant principals. We have chosen to use only one title simply to reduce the complexity of the text. We are also aware that not all principals will experience contextual pressures in the particular ways in which they are discussed. The experience of these pressures will vary depending on race, socioeconomic status, class, etc.

3. Our survey methods involved using two overlapping questionnaires. These questionnaires were completed during staff gatherings, and the participants were given the option of remaining anonymous. The first contained mostly open-ended questions, where

teachers were asked, for instance, about the general pressures experienced. In answering the survey, most teachers did not have the time to detail an exhaustive list of all the pressures they experienced. It is likely that they mostly reflected on that which was salient in their experience that particular day or week. As researchers, it is a choice that we made to first ask open-ended questions to our participants in order to gather a broader range of ideas. The second questionnaire was a multiple-choice version that covered similar content area. It was interesting to contrast the response generated through free writing with the response from a more structured question.

4. Unfortunately, antagonistic relationships between the union and administrators add to these problems as tasks and responsibilities become so rigidly and narrowly defined that the possibility of being flexible and adapt to the changing realities of life becomes eliminated.

CHAPTER TWO

Creating an Environment for Change

Obviously you cannot change the broader cultural context and general expectations for educators. To a certain extent you can have a *local* effect in the subculture of your school, and we will discuss that in a subsequent section on school culture (Chapter 6). However, if you truly understand that specific contexts and cultures can pressure everyone into nonpreferred ways of being, it then becomes completely logical to talk about staff problems in an externalized way. In other words, if the context prevents people from functioning in a preferred and helpful way, then the problem can be talked about as coming from outside the person.

Externalization of problems is a fundamental concept in the Narrative Approach. This practice, developed by Michael White (White & Epston, 1990), is based on the idea that problems, just like unwanted habits, may develop because of a series of life circumstances. Externalizing a problem implies that it is perceived as distinct from the person's identity. As such, an individual will not be talked about as an "angry person" but rather as someone struggling with anger or disrespect. In many ways, this practice resembles the medical model of helping a well-intentioned person manage allergies or anxiety. People often experience problems as being out of their control even if it may not seem so to an observer. By externalizing problems, we recognize that problems are not indicative of who others want to be, but are reactions they can learn to escape from and control.

Talking about problems in externalized ways has several major impacts:

- It shifts people's perspectives in profound ways. Instead of hating themselves, they suddenly start hating the problem. Externalizing promotes *hope and agency*. In this process, a *space* is created where people are less weighed down, less paralyzed, and more able to take action against the "habit" of, for example, bullying and disrespect. (Although the word *habit* is incongruent with the cultural and post-structuralist conceptualization of the narrative approach, it can be useful in actual conversations with young people as long as we remain connected with the more accurate guiding concepts.)

- When a problem is externalized, it becomes a tangible entity that is nameable, contained, and clear. This new perspective allows people to *take a stand against "it"* and *take responsibility* for their behaviors of disrespect and bullying (often for the first time). People learn to control "it" as opposed to "it" controlling them. In other words, externalization makes the effects of the problem more visible, enhances the necessity of taking action, and renders people more capable of making different choices to change their lives.

- As the community starts seeing the problem as a separate entity, everyone starts noticing people's special talents, values, and intentions. The focus shifts from blaming people to working as a *team* and noticing people's efforts against problems.

The externalization of problems is often difficult to grasp at first. A good way to understand this concept is to apply it to your own life and consider, for example, your personal relationship to impatience. Many of you may recall having done or said something at school under the influence of impatience that did not quite fit with how you prefer to be. Later on, you may even have regretted your actions, felt guilty, and promised yourself not to do that again. Imagine, however, someone talking about you as an impatient person, and this becoming part of your reputation. This might trigger more frustration and a sense of being misunderstood or misrepresented. This *frustration in itself* would increase the likelihood that you'd engage in "impatient" behaviors again even if you did not want to. In other words, the way the problem is talked about will in itself create a context of resentment in which the problem is more likely to happen again.

Now imagine having externalized impatience. You would create a thorough list of effects that impatience might have on multiple aspects of your life; you would notice when it takes over and when it does not, and what it gets you to do, think, or feel that is against your preference. You might eventually be frustrated *at* the problematic aspects of impatience and make a decision that, given its effects, you do not want to let it rule you in those particular ways anymore. Through supportive externalizing conversation, you might identify the first signs that may lead up to an impatience problem and explore ways of going in a preferred direction. In a simplified way, this process of articulating, noticing, and making choices about the effects of the problem and simultaneously about the way you prefer to act will ultimately allow you to take responsibility, be clearer about personally relevant options, and have preferred experiences of yourself in difficult interactions.

EXERCISE: EXTERNALIZATION

Chose a problem that has affected you at school. It can be anything, such as an emotion (anger, anxiety, impatience, depression, frustration, self-hate, boredom, distrust, fear, shyness, discouragement, etc.), a thought (self-criticism or critical voice, blaming, perfectionism, comparison, self-doubt, evaluation, ambition, etc.), or a habit or behavioral pattern (sarcasm, interrupting, dominating, rushing, irresponsibility, disrespect, etc.). Explore how this problem has affected you in the past and how you've seen it affect other people by answering these questions.

1. How does _____ affect you?

   _____

   _____

2. What does _____ make you do, say, think, and feel?

   Do: _____

   Say: _____

   Think: _____

   Feel: _____

3. When and how did you first notice _____?

   _____

   _____

4. How does _____ affect your relationships?

   _____

   _____

5. How does _____ make you feel about yourself?

_____

_____

6. When are you *most likely* to resist _____?

_____

_____

7. Can you remember an example this past week where you could have given into _____ but didn't? What did you do to avoid _____? What were you thinking and doing as the situation evolved?

_____

_____

Externalization is not a technique that you use on people. A technique is a method, a procedure that you use to manipulate people into certain positions. For an externalization to be helpful, it has to be embedded in conversations that reflect its fundamental implications. The goal in externalizing conversations is to clearly support others in the face of their struggle; express the philosophy that people are constrained by contexts, patterns of interactions, and habitual reactions; and communicate that we know there is more to any individual than the problem. If one uses an externalization but maintains a blaming and personalizing attitude, the outcome of the conversation will not be any different. Given the importance of attitude, we will now distinguish deficit-focused assumptions in problem-solving conversation and the externalizing stance we are promoting in this book.

By "deficit-focused" we mean the process of:

1. Observing and Gathering Data on the Problem

Principals and educators are often trained to pay particular attention to the details that fit in certain diagnostic categories of pathology. This follows the deficit model of analysis where professionals are supposed to correct deficits instead of building on existing competence. This can be overwhelming and discouraging to educators. For example: A principal might wonder if a teacher has good control over students and scrutinize that teacher often in a way that is likely to cause unease to the teacher and support the assumption.

2. Comparing Your Perception of the Problem to Your Criteria of Normality

Principals and educators are often trained to observe and document thoughts, feelings, and behavior (in a vacuum) of staff and students to compare them to predetermined criteria of "normality." The goal then becomes to use various strategies to bring people closer to this "normality," which is often biased by the dominant culture and disregards the contextual constraints of the lives of staff and students. For example: A principal may be concerned about a teacher's mannerism and interprets it negatively without regard for the teacher's cultural background.

3. Making Assumptions

People's minds will often naturally fill in the blanks, and this becomes very dangerous if people are in positions of power, such as principals, and do not verify assumptions. This mind-filling can lead to principals ascribing meaning to the lives of staff and students as opposed to being respectful and empowering them to articulate their own preferred versus nonpreferred meanings. For example: A teacher may leave the staff meeting early because of family obligations and may be perceived as lazy and uncommitted to her career, while in reality she is very invested in both career and family life.

4. Fixing the Problem

Pressure is placed on principals to "fix" teachers and students. This inadvertently creates a hierarchy where principals can overanalyze problems and become disconnected from people as people. For example: A principal may decide to micromanage staff when perceiving that teachers are behind schedule.

Externalizing is not congruent with this stance as it implies the following:

1. There is more to people than their problems. Believing in the richness of people's ways of being allows for more *compassion*. For example: The principal assumes that a teacher has good intentions and is competent when faced with an issue.

2. Criteria of normality omit the many nuances of background, cultural diversity, and *contexts* of lives. For example: Staff can be invited to discuss how their social class backgrounds affect their interactions with children and parents and whether their policies are realistic given the culture of the school population.

3. An important goal of externalizing is assisting people to articulate their preferred way of being as different from their problem. This implies a certain *curiosity* about the invisible yet preferred aspects of others. For example: A principal could be intrigued by a teacher's ideas about discipline, his intentions, goals, and instances when he handled a situation in a way that was helpful to students.

4. Externalization places the responsibility of addressing the problem on the protagonist, as individuals are the best judges of their own lives. The principal is clearly there to support the process, *collaborate,* and participate as a team member, but does not dominate the process. For example: A principal can reduce hierarchy by giving teachers the opportunity to lead various staff meetings and make important decisions.

COMPARING DEFICIT-FOCUSED VERSUS CONTEXTUALIZED UNDERSTANDING

Summary of the 4 "C's" of Helpful Conversation

Comparative Table of Deficit-Focused Attitude Versus a Contextualized Understanding

Selective Attention to Problem	*Compassion: Acknowledge the Richness of People*
Educators are often trained to pay particular attention to the details that fit in certain diagnostic categories of problems or pathology. This follows the deficit model of analysis where professionals are supposed to correct deficits instead of building on existing competence. This can be overwhelming and discouraging to all.	Believing that people are really oppressed by these pressures and problems, and that there is another more preferred version of that same individual which is caring and successful and with whom it is possible to connect.
Comparing Your Perception of the Problem to Your Criteria of Normality	*Contextualized Perspective*
Educators are often trained to observe and document people's thoughts, feelings and behavior (in a vacuum) to compare them to predetermined criteria of "normality." The goal then becomes to use various strategies to bring people closer to this "normality," which is often biased by the dominant culture and disregards the contextual constraints of people's lives.	• Keeping in mind the broader context • Thinking at a meta level of the larger sociocultural perspective (gender, class, etc.) • Deconstructing or examining influences on individuals' responses to a situation and challenging beliefs in our own minds, communities, and dominant culture that simplify human behavior.

Making Assumptions	Curiosity About the Invisible Complexity of Others' Lives
People's minds will often naturally fill the blanks; this becomes very dangerous if people are in positions of power, such as principals, and do not verify assumptions. This mind-filling leads to educators ascribing meaning to people's lives as opposed to being respectful and empowering them to articulate their own preferred vs. nonpreferred meanings.	Adults and children are considered experts in their own experiences. Professionals' expertise lies in the ability to ask *helpful questions* and explore new possibilities by taking a genuine "not knowing" stance and being intrigued by a person's thoughts, values, hopes, and dreams. Focus is much broader than the problem in an attempt to identify the ingredients of preferred experiences.

Expert: Fix the Problem	Collaboration and Empowerment
Pressure is placed on principals to "fix" problems and people. This inadvertently creates a hierarchy where the principal can overanalyze problems and become disconnected from people as people. It can also leave the protagonist less actively involved in taking responsibilities for change.	Principals seek to minimize power imbalance between them as professionals and teachers. Given that most people have struggled with some form of disqualification in their lives, it is important that the process provide a forum for conversations that do not replicate contributing factors to problems.

Application: An Externalized Conversation Between a Principal and Teacher[1]

Principal Suzanne Hughes is concerned about the behavior of tenured teacher Alice Stevens during meetings. Alice has been making sarcastic comments, sighing dramatically, and using body language to show her disapproval or scorn for comments or suggestions from colleagues. Suzanne has noticed the effects, such as teachers' reluctance to speak up and meetings being less generative of creative ideas. As principal, Suzanne feels this is the most difficult aspect of her job: dealing with a staff member who acts in a negative and demoralizing way. She has asked Alice to meet with her after school. These two have worked together in the same school for a number of years. She prepares herself mentally for the conversation and takes a deep breath.

Example of an Externalized Principal-Teacher Dialogue

Alice: (knock, knock)

Suzanne: Hi Alice, please come in. I appreciate you agreeing to meet with me.	Starting the meeting with an acknowledgment of the effort.
Alice: It's OK, Suzanne. I have a lot to do, but I have some time.	
Suzanne: I have been wanting to talk to you because I am concerned about the atmosphere at the staff meetings. I am wondering . . . how are the staff meetings for you?	Suzanne is transparent about her concerns and puts the focus on the context of the problem: the staff meeting. She also approaches the issue with a stance of respectful curiosity rather than blame. She conveys that she is interested in the actual experience of her teacher, which in some ways implies that she knows Alice can be a different person.
Alice: Well, they are productive, but a little long . . . and boring.	
Suzanne: I really try to make them as short as possible. Can you help me understand what makes them boring?	Keeping the focus or blame on the context (staff meeting) and inviting Alice into a description of its effect on her.

Alice: I've got so much to do, and to have to sit and listen to naive questions and people discussing subjects like photocopying or playground rules for 30 minutes really takes it out of me.

Suzanne: What effect do these conversations have on you? (pause) When they happen you end up, what, . . . frustrated? Resentful? . . .

Having established a collaborative, compassionate, nonblaming-defensive pattern of conversation, Suzanne gently moves to externalizing a problem that develops for Alice in the context of staff meetings.

Alice: Well, frankly, it makes me angry and resentful that my time is being used up.

Suzanne: So some Anger and Resentment creeps in and it makes you feel like you're wasting precious time?

Suzanne externalizes the problems described by Alice, being careful to use Alice's names for her experience (anger and resentment); she also restates what Alice just said to make sure she understood correctly and to let Alice know that she is following her experience.

Alice: Yeah . . .

Suzanne: Have Anger and Resentment been creeping in more and more for you in the recent staff meetings than those at the beginning of the year? It seems like it to me . . .

Suzanne makes clear to Alice that she knows Alice is not at her best lately by conveying to her that she has noticed her on other, more constructive occasions. In other words, she reassures Alice that she sees more than just the problem and that she is aware that it is probably not Alice's preferred way of being.

(Continued)

(Continued)

Alice: Definitely.

Suzanne: I've noticed that in district meetings that Resentment and Impatience get me to act in ways I don't like, like raising my voice. Do you have an idea of what Resentment gets you to focus on during staff meetings?

Suzanne *genuinely* states that she has been affected by similar problems as well, which has the effects of: (1) Fostering collaboration and minimizing any hierarchy or unfavorable comparison/evaluation that could distance them in this moment of sharing; (2) Acknowledging that problems such as Resentment push everyone away from their preferred ways of being; this furthers the externalization, demarginalizes the teacher, and opens space to talk about more unwanted behaviors. Note that Suzanne in her personal sharing does not move away from the focus of the conversation; she shares the minimum necessary to create a sense of companionship in the experience without asking for support from Alice.

Alice: It gets me to watch the clock to see how many minutes are wasted, and it gets me to say something to help people move onto the next subject so that we can get done faster.

Suzanne: OK, so it gets you to want to move faster? (Alice nods) Yes, your comments do make people quieter and ready to move on, in my

Suzanne invites Alice into a noticing of the effects of Resentment on many areas of her life: effects on the meeting, relationship, and reputation.

observation. But do you have a guess on how this Resentment affects others, your relationship with them, and how they might perceive you?

Alice: I have friends here who know who I really am, but there are probably people who misunderstand me.

Suzanne: Where is this Resentment going to take your relationship with your colleagues?

Suzanne continues to map the effects of the problem in areas that are relevant to the situation. These questions are regrouped and condensed here, but would usually be spread in time and space to progressively and gently include effects on self, thoughts, feelings, school culture, and so forth.

Alice: I hadn't thought about that. I assume it will pass, that we'll get along.

Suzanne: Well, how does Resentment affect how you feel about yourself as a colleague? Does this align with the hopes you had for this year?

Alice: I'd have to think about it.

Suzanne: OK, but just think of how this Resentment affects the quality of the decisions made in our meetings.

(Continued)

(Continued)

Alice: They are made faster.

Suzanne: That's partially true; I wonder in the long run, if our decisions are rushed, we might end up with more meetings to go over the repercussions of decisions. Or we may have to take more time to revisit the issues later. For example, I have felt like I ought to bring back the computer lab issue because not everyone contributed an opinion.

Still exploring the effects of Resentment and Anger. Often, exploring the effects of a problem will make visible the fact that it has the opposite effect of that which was intended.

Alice: I hadn't thought about that . . . so the Resentment might actually bring more of what I try to avoid . . .

Suzanne: It's been my impression that it does. . . .

Suzanne: I know you work really hard and are committed to our community; I really appreciate that. It makes me wonder if there are other things going on that you feel comfortable sharing with me or that I can help with?

Suzanne conveys her awareness and appreciation for the "other side" of Alice, or, in narrative terms, her preferred self. She then proceeds to inquire about other potential contextual factors that may contribute to Alice not being her preferred self. Although she is aware that Alice may not share personal matters with her as an employer, it will at least give Alice an experience of being supported and understood.

Alice: My family life is kinda hectic right now. It's giving me a short fuse.

Suzanne: That must be hard. Is that something you want to talk about, or is there something I can do to help?

Suzanne expresses genuine compassion, knowing from her own experience how difficult it is to balance school and family issues. As for Alice, receiving compassion can in itself contribute to lowering the problem of Resentment. In making her feel more connected with her principal, the resulting context of the staff meeting is slightly shifted to one where she's not simply dealing with Anger and Resentment alone in her little corner.

Alice: No. Thanks, but that's fine.

Suzanne: Last year, I remember that you shared some struggles as well and yet I experienced you as participating more in staff meetings discussions. What is it that kept you going then?

Suzanne recalls times that were challenging and when Resentment and Anger could have taken over but didn't. She assists Alice in articulating what it was that might have helped her avoid Resentment then. In other words, she helps Alice articulate her very own strategies and the ingredients of her previous successes in avoiding the problem. By doing this Suzanne avoids the pitfall of giving advice, which is almost always ineffective in the lives of others.

Alice: Hmm . . . that's an interesting question. I had forgotten about that. I think maybe serving as a mentor teacher helped me understand their struggles and kept me connected with their needs for these discussions.

(Continued)

(Continued)

Suzanne: So Resentment and Anger are disconnecting you from that understanding?

Alice: I guess . . . I really don't want that to happen . . . (sigh) I'll try to keep Resentment to myself . . .

Suzanne: Is there something I can do in staff meetings to actually help you push away Resentment or even shrink it?

Suzanne again wants to offer her support and see if the context can be changed in a way that invites less Resentment.

Alice: I'm not sure; you could keep people on the subject . . .

Suzanne; I've got an idea . . . would you like to help me out in staff meetings by being a timekeeper for our agenda, or you could help me co-facilitate a meeting? I would really value your help.

Suzanne recruits the assistance of Alice. She is hoping to create a context that will bring forth Alice's preferred ways of being and special talents. When a voice is loud in staff meetings, it is often helpful to recruit the person's assistance in making other voices heard or in co-facilitating a more constructive process. Suzanne also genuinely values the involvement of her staff.

In this conversation, Suzanne holds onto the notion that there is a problem affecting Alice and pushing her away from her preferred self. In other words, Suzanne is connected at all times to the fact that people are affected in ways they don't like by problems and contexts, and consequently have multiple selves.

A Question From Educators: What do you mean by "multiple selves"? How do you know who someone really is?

Who Is the Real Person? How Can We Tell?

From a narrative point of view, people have many selves. One self is no more *real* than another. . . . This statement is contradictory to many popular psychology handbooks and traditional Western philosophies that assume a core personality.

People's experiences of themselves are constructed in relationships and evolve over time (Gergen, 1985, 1991; Hoffman, 1990). Relationships, particularly if they are with people having a significant influence over one's life, provide the canvas for the meaning making of experience. In other words, we could argue that a person who lived in a vacuum would have a very limited sense of self, if any, as no one would be affected by his or her presence, and no one would be available to reflect back their experience of that person. This individual would have no basis for experiencing him- or herself as clever or funny, for example, without an interaction with another being allowing the individual to ascribe that interpretation to those particular ways of being.

If the self is constructed in relationships, then each individual has multiple selves that reflect different experiences of self-in-relationships. These different selves exist in the past, present, and future, and particular versions of them are brought to the forefront of experience by the context and the presence of certain people in a certain space. Among the many possible selves, some are preferred to others in terms of their effects on relationships and their congruency with one's intentions (and others are less preferred). For instance, many people experience themselves as shy in certain relationships and very outgoing in others.

Similarly, teachers can be experienced as very kind and patient in certain relationships and very impatient in others. In fact, many educators come across students who give radically different stories about who a teacher is. It is quite common to have a person engage in behaviors that may appear contradictory in terms of the person's intentions. In reality, these are simply different versions of selves that are brought forth by the context. The only influence others can have is to engage people in a reflection and assist them in understanding, articulating, and eventually choosing which self is more in line with who they prefer to be. The concept of multiple selves is complex and confusing to many, especially those more familiar with popular psychology. Let us further explore this concept and its implications in the stories of your own life with an exercise.

EXERCISE: PROBLEM-SATURATED VERSUS PREFERRED STORY OF EDUCATORS' LIVES

1. Most people have faced challenges at work. In the following space, write four sentences about things you have done at school that you may not be proud of or that could be judged negatively by your colleagues:

_____

_____

_____

_____

2. In the following space, please write four sentences about a reputation or story that could have started circulating about

you at school if someone were to link the events listed in No. 1 and ascribe a negative meaning:

_____

_____

_____

_____

3. Now write four sentences about actions you took at school that you are most proud of and that reflect your true values and intentions:

_____

_____

_____

_____

4. Write four sentences describing the reputation or story that has or could have followed from someone noticing these actions and ascribing a positive meaning to them:

_____

_____

_____

_____

Notice that you have just written two different stories about yourself, one that is saturated with a negative focus and one that is more in line with how you truly prefer to be as an educator. Which is the real you? This question becomes pointless because these may be just different facets of you in different contexts. The actions you took in No. 1 may have taken place at times when you felt pressured to be a good role model, to be overly dedicated or appear in complete control, or you were simply overwhelmed, stressed, and tired. The actions you took in No. 3 may have happened when you were more connected with your intentions and/or when the context was one of confidence, appreciation, and self-reflection (such contexts are discussed in more depth in Chapter 6).

When applied to ourselves, this process makes visible the fact that most people experience their intentions and positive ways of being as being their true self. Our culture tends to support the concept that others' "true selves" are negative ones. This is especially the case when we are in a position of power and are evaluating others. There is often incongruence in how we determine who one's very own true self is versus who another's true self is (note that when people experience self-doubt, problems get them to think of their true self as the negative one). We would like to take these ideas a step farther and propose that even the concept of a true self is not accurate in that in reality people have many selves. What then becomes important is which self is preferred and what context is likely to bring this self forward.

In other words, every person can be seen as a reservoir of multiple ways of being. Context will often influence or determine which way of being becomes expressed, and this sometimes fosters the development of problems. This is particularly true if people attempt to be a way that doesn't fit for them or the context. Through helpful conversations, individuals can be invited to articulate what their preferred way of being is, how to access it more often, and how to shelter themselves from the context.

5. Summary: Write one line about a problem-saturated story and another about your preferred story:

Problem-saturated story:

_____

Preferred story:

_____

As you can imagine, you can write a story that presents all the people you know in quite a negative light or bring forth a perspective about their intentions, values, or effort that makes them knights in shining armor. Those multiple facets of people are always there. Sometimes people get trapped in the contexts of their lives and engage mostly in unhelpful actions, as in problem stories. Our goal in this book is to help you believe that the other version of this same person exists, find ways to support your compassion enough to create a context where this preferred educator may come forth, be his or her best, and contribute to your staff.

In general, it can be said that *perspective is the antidote to most problems*. Problems tend to narrow our views.[2] Understanding and gaining perspective makes visible many options that were initially in the shadow.

SUMMARY OF THE PRACTICE OF EXTERNALIZING AND RESTORYING

Summary of Basic Considerations in the Externalization of a Problem

Externalizing	*Comments*
A problem that is experienced as a feeling, behavior, or thought can be talked about as an external entity:	Make sure that you use people's words for describing their own experiences.

(Continued)

(Continued)

- Feelings: What did this "Anger" want you to do?
- Behavior: When "Blaming" happened, how did you feel inside?
- Thought: Is "Self-doubt" most likely to sneak into your mind at recess or in class?

If people focus on external events (e.g., another teacher), first thoroughly acknowledge the difficulties of the experience; then, when people are sufficiently heard, bring gently into the conversation the effect that this event might have had on them and what they might end up doing that they would rather not do.

Map the effects of the chosen externalization on all areas of life (feelings; thoughts; behaviors; identity; relationships with parents, teachers, and friends; hopes; dreams; activities; performances; sleeping; eating, etc.).

Make sure that you are in touch with people's experience and are not simply bombarding them with a redundant formulated effect question.

Statement of position: Invite individuals to reflect upon the effects and decide if they want to change the situation.

Leave yourself open to curiosity if, after reflection, people say they do not want to take a stand against the problem. Explore the costs and benefits (if any) of the problem and whether there are other ways to get the same benefits with less cost.

Unique outcomes: Notice and discuss the events and intentions that lay outside of the problem story, such as moments of success at functioning without the problem.

Preferred story: Link several moments of success together and explore the meaning of their increasing occurrence.

This simply becomes another map of effects, except that this time it is about the effects of the successes.

A Question From Educators: Will externalizing a problem remove a person's responsibility to deal with it?

Externalizing increases people's responsibility to deal with issues. Externalizing simply conveys to people that we see problems as not representative of who they can and may prefer to be. Externalizing sends a message of hope and support that allows people to articulate the effects of problems, develop an understanding of why they personally would want to change their connection to this problem, and notice their own capacity to be successfully different.

NOTES

1. The timing, sequencing, and appropriateness of these questions can be very variable depending on context (!!) and relationship. This conversation is reconstructed and abbreviated and is not meant to be taken as a recipe for difficult conversation but rather as one of many examples of helpful conversation.

2. For example, frustration often gets people to dwell on an upsetting event and be oblivious to the rest of the day and the bigger picture of the situation.

CHAPTER THREE

Typical School Culture Problems and Their Effects

I n this section we will explore the issues that contribute to common school culture problems. These problems are believed to result mostly from the context in which people and schools are embedded. For this reason, as elsewhere in the book, these problems will generally be externalized.

The most frequently mentioned problems[1] in school staff cultures, as well as their contributors and effects on school culture, will be covered. When staff cohesiveness is negatively impacted, nothing can really function at its best and everyone suffers, adults and children. This is clearly articulated by the following principal:

> *When teachers are not happy, then they don't work well together, the morale goes down, they're grumpy, and it shows in every-thing everybody does. The kids are affected. When teachers are not happy, they are rather dull and boring in front of a classroom.*

> —Elementary School Principal

Solutions and practices that can be used to avoid or solve these problems will be presented in Chapter 6.

Gossip

The Gossip habit recruits people into repeating information or rumors about someone, usually in a covert manner. It may provide a sense of power due to the telling and receiving of a secret, which can generate an experience of complicity and belonging. Remember the last time gossip reached your ears. How did it make you feel? Many people report that gossip gives them a sense of status and honor to be trusted and included in the exchange. This can be particularly appealing when people experience discontent and powerlessness in their general work situation. Gossip can be present to various degrees with different levels of effects. A contained gossip habit that is only occasional and has very little effect on the community is almost unavoidable in very large schools and districts. However, if it is constant and negatively impacts staff cohesiveness and trust, it can become dangerous.

Gossip About Teachers

Gossip is more likely to strike teachers when they have limited opportunities to bond and share openly meaningful aspects of their private life. It can also occur when distrust and criticism dominate a staff climate. If meaningful aspects of teachers' lives are not shared openly, the Gossip habit will make sure they are shared secretly. When the gossiping and judging habits occur, they ironically reduce the likelihood that people will share openly in the future. A vicious cycle of distrust, judgment, and secrecy is established between different subgroups of teachers. One educator commented,

> I really hate it when I hear a teacher talk about people's personal lives in a way that makes you wonder what they say about you when you aren't there.

Gossip may also occasionally get a principal to repeat confidential information to trusted teachers. This is more likely to occur when principals feel isolated and have few out-of-school confidants with whom to process their concerns. Ironically, however, this gossip habit just fuels more isolation for the principals, as the staff, even the confidants, can become distrustful and ambivalent about sharing personal information, as revealed by the following teacher:

I love our principal—she has many, many strengths and is very respected by our staff and community. However, the one complaint I've had about her is that she can be loose-lipped and prone to gossip. I don't have a horror story, fortunately. I just feel that she often relays too much personal information to other confidants and me about fellow staff members and district people.

Gossip can be the result of problem stories or can evolve into a powerful problem story so alienating that a teacher may feel that she has no option other than leaving.

I was in a situation that led to very horrible results. We had a principal for five years that was undermining staff members and causing people not to trust each other. She would pit one teacher against another. Even after she left, the results lingered. There was one teacher who was so mean to me and stayed that way, even after the climate changed under a new principal. I did try going to her to solve it, but, finally, I decided I couldn't take it anymore. I asked for a transfer to another school.

—First Grade Teacher

Gossip About Principals

Gossip gets teachers to spread stories about principals when a genuine relationship does not exist between the principal and the staff. From our research, it seems that this problem is more likely to occur when people are upset about or misunderstand an administrative decision, when differences of opinion dominate a situation, or when an "us-them" relationship with the administration has been established. For some people, a certain amount of gossip is understandable and acceptable because of the power differential of the principal and the limited personal contact between teachers and principal. As mentioned earlier, a small Gossip habit is often expected about isolated events or an occasional unpopular decision. Dangerous problems can grow, however, if Gossip contributes to the spreading of an elaborate problem story about the principal as a person. When a problem story like this develops, it can seriously interfere with the principal's credibility and the staff's cohesiveness. It also reduces the staff's willingness to follow the principal as a leader, explore novel educational experiences, and trust any invitations for change. The school community can become divided by this problem, polarized between those who believe in the problem identity and those who perceive their principal's actions in a different light (see Chapter 4 for the solving of such situations). The principal may also develop a problem story about the staff and may resort to gestures of power that may increase the distrust, as opposed to solving the misrepresentations. As discussed earlier, problem stories take on a life of their own when people notice only events that can justify or fit into a particular problem story.

In our research, a principal shared with us an unfortunate situation in which a staff member afflicted with a Gossip habit interpreted the principal's joy as being related to the resignation of a teacher, when in reality it was because of completely separate good news. This teacher then proceeded to spread the rumor that the principal was celebrating the departure of a fellow staff person. Fortunately, in this situation, the principal was able to pull the teacher out of class, explain the situation, and demand that the building gossip be clarified immediately.

At its worst, this problem can get staff to spend a lot of energy undermining principals. Meanwhile, principals spend a lot of energy defending and trying to prove themselves and, under pressure, may resort to decisions that may fuel the problem story. Sometimes attempts at solving the problem, whether by the use of power or by self-revelation, only further thicken the problem story.

When a Gossip habit is seriously spreading in a school, its general effects are to

- Reduce the likelihood of collaboration
- Increase isolation
- Create a judgmental and distrustful environment
- Generate misrepresentations and resentments

PROBLEM-SATURATED CONVERSATION

It really saddens me when I see fellow teachers treat students with disrespect. They yell and embarrass them in public and say negative comments. They usually just complain without trying to change the situation.

—Elementary School Teacher

It really gets to me when a teacher makes a judgment, has a negative attitude, and makes assumptions about my students before knowing ALL the facts.

—Elementary School Teacher

I only hear the complaints. For example, I had a teacher who stayed at school from 5–7 P.M. the night before Valentine's Day. This was so parents could come leave special valentines, which their child would receive in the morning. No parent came to acknowledge what a beautiful, over-the-top gesture this was! I only heard about it from the librarian.

—Elementary School Principal

Conversations between teacher and teacher, principal and teacher, parent and teacher, principal and parent, and parent and parent are predominantly based around problems. On school campuses, people discuss everything from budget problems to running out of paper to gossiping to discussing students' and parents' perceived problems. In the morning, a well-discussed session about how to deal with the outdated computer lab may occur. At recess, two teachers may touch base on the behavioral issues of a student. Often this is done in the public staff room with other teachers listening. A lunchtime discussion about union issues may involve many teachers. After school a teacher may have to call several parents about problems in the classroom, meet with the principal regarding a negative evaluation, and then journey back to the classroom to answer numerous e-mails and phone messages about student issues.

My first teaching job in Massachusetts was dominated by negative chatter. I felt I had to be enthusiastic and creative in secret. Eventually it wore me down to such a degree I (like it does the majority of them) even took up smoking cigarettes! Ugh!

—Elementary School Teacher

Even though the problem focus is present in many kinds of exchanges, it seems to particularly dominate in conversations about students. In that sense, Problem Talk about students has truly evolved into a school habit that leaves adults so comfortable talking about children in a negative way that it is done openly, with or without the student present. This habit may lure adults into a belief that they are connecting with each other on common ground (since everyone is familiar with that style of conversation).

Problem-saturated conversations particularly thrive in the staff room when teachers accumulate frustrations or become exhausted because of all the responsibilities and demands on their time. Teachers generally give a lot of thought and energy to their students and do not necessarily receive much appreciation from the community. Furthermore, there can be a sense that nothing is ever good enough, as you can always learn more, improve, or take care of someone's needs. Frustration can easily grow in that context and, coupled with the scarcity of time, create a perfect setting for Problem Talk.

Problem-saturated communications can become serious problems in schools. First, teachers suffer from a negative drain of energy. Not only is precious time spent receiving/giving negativity, but in the meantime teachers are not receiving refreshing positive energy. In addition, you never have a break from work if you talk about work during breaks. This focus on negativity can breed more negativity, as there is always something to be dissatisfied about. The whole atmosphere can become one of focusing on the glass being half empty. In such a context, only superficial connections can develop among teachers. If teachers spend much of their time dwelling on negative aspects of their work, there is no time left to discover each other's talents and uniqueness and to enrich their sense of community.

Second, Problem Talk may recruit teachers into speculating with each other about the cause of students' issues. This typically feeds the common problem story of parents or internal deficiencies as the "cause" of student problems and can seriously inhibit the precious collaboration between all the important parties in a student's life, which unfortunately thwarts a team effort to promote a child's well-being. We do not deny that family struggles have an effect on students, but rather we simply question the often quick assessment of parents as being "dysfunctional." It often seems a ready-made problem-saturated explanation for most problems.

Third, problem-saturated communication locks students into problem reputations or stories. Problem reputations limit student changes because people usually notice only problem events. Teachers also become locked into a static problem story that may blind them to student growth.

Unlike the Gossip habit, where individuals are fully conscious of engaging in a frowned-upon disrespectful exchange, problem-saturated conversations about kids are often unrestricted by social conventions. Why would bad-mouthing an adult be offensive and covert, while bad-mouthing students be commonplace and public? People may sometimes justify this type of conversation by assuming that it will help them deal better with the student later. The distinction between problem-saturated conversation and helpful consultations with colleagues, however, lies in the effects they generate. A professional consultation with a colleague is usually done privately, may include more objective, factual information about the situation, a description of the student as a whole person, and the teacher's inadvertent contributions to the problem. Such focused and honest conversations can be very valuable in generating ideas, especially if they remain respectful of the student. Problem-saturated conversations, however, are often one sided and focus mainly on the student, who is perceived as "the problem." While the teacher may feel some immediate relief through the mere sharing and talking about the problem, in the long run it often simply increases the problem reputation of the child (especially when it is done openly, in front of everyone). The increasingly negative focus on the child recruits more people into noticing and interpreting the child's behavior in a problem way and consequently punishing small incidents that would otherwise have been unnoticed or discounted. A problem story or perception of the child that is biased by the struggle and that makes preferred moments invisible generally increases students' unhappiness and frustration, which in turn contributes to more problem behavior.

CLIQUES

Cliques essentially develop in a context of differences. The staff may be too heterogeneous to understand each other, may not have enough time to process their differences, may carry unresolved conflicts, or may simply lack the opportunities to bridge and discover the values of differences in a safe way. Cliques can develop based on similarities, such as years of teaching experience, strict adherence to a specification, career goals, family orientation, religious affiliation, ethnic identity, race, educational philosophies, and more. Cliques offer a sense of familiarity, belonging, and exclusivity.

When I first joined my last district I felt like Goldilocks in The Three Bears. *The first group I sat with for lunch was "too hard." They were cynical, negative, and (though very friendly to me, at the time I perceived them as) quite cliquish. The second group was "too soft"—I thought each person was so uneducated I couldn't imagine how they managed to get a teaching degree. The third group was "just right" for me! We laughed, we gossiped, we complained, we shared ideas, personal stories, discussed politics, etcetera. I loved this group. I thought each person was smart, interesting, thoughtful, funny, and a good teacher. Sometimes we needed to "vent." We supported each other when any one of numerous aspects of teaching public school got us down. It lifted our spirits to spend lunchtime together, as I believe each teacher group lifted its members' spirits. Sometimes you need to feel you're not alone with your frustrations.*

—Elementary School Teacher

Everyone needs the support of close colleagues to share intimate aspects of life and lift their spirits. Cliques both overlap with and are distinct from friendships. The difference between close friendships and cliques is that membership in a clique often implies *disconnection* from the community. Specifically, Cliques may require that their members eat together (sometimes in a secluded place like a classroom), exclude nonmembers from socializing activities, and repeat unhelpful gossip about other members of the community. Cliques are often toxic to a school environment, as they prevent collaboration and the sharing of ideas.

Cliques thwart the richness of diversity, stifle creativity, and make it particularly hard for new teachers to feel welcome and to become contributing members of the team.

When I was new on a school campus, people didn't know who I was nor did they try to find out. I would look around at lunch for someone to eat with, but everyone was eating in their classrooms, either working alone during lunch or eating and chatting in small, impenetrable groups. By November, I was eating alone and contemplating moving to a new school!

—Fourth Grade Teacher

The Us-Them Attitude

Historically, unions were created to protect the rights of the worker. By the 21st century, the conditions of employees in most areas had greatly improved, due in part to the existence of unions. In fields such as education, where employees are typically overworked and underpaid, the presence of a union makes a lot of sense.

In certain districts, union representatives collaborate respectfully with administrators and simply do their work of protecting teachers' rights.

> *My experience is that the union is extremely helpful. They serve as an advocate for teachers on numerous levels. They defend teachers' rights to have a fair wage, good working conditions, and fair evaluations. I personally have never had experience with "a union going too far." I do know of a case where they offered support and advocated on behalf of a very ineffectual teacher who was on the brink of being fired. She had taught in the district for over 40 years. At one time she had been a won-derful teacher. Though I thought she was a bad teacher, I was glad the union was making sure she was being treated respectfully and fairly.*
>
> —Retired Elementary School Teacher

Unfortunately, since negotiations have frequently been of an antagonistic nature, some union representatives have diverged from the position of protecting to one of fighting everything. In other words, what would normally be a side effect of negotiation (conflicting relationships with an employer) becomes a habit in and of itself, promoting an us-them attitude. This position erroneously promotes the idea that administrators are "enemies" who intend to take advantage of their staff. Moreover, the habit of fighting may represent the feelings of only a small group of teachers, leaving many others in the uncomfortable position of not agreeing with those supposedly there to represent them!

Union services are structured differently in different districts. In some districts, union leaders are simply teachers who chose to engage in this additional function. This may offer the advantage of the union representative knowing more about teachers on each school site. However, we can question the objectivity of representatives who are simultaneously part of a teaching staff. In many professions this corresponds to a dual-role relationship[2] and is considered unethical. In other districts, union leaders maintain their objectivity by not being attached to a particular school.

In our union, we have objective people who do not work on any school site, so they can help facilitate resolution. If two educators can't stand each other or don't see what the other sees, we have a conversation between all parties, list all options, and then take actions based on these actions. We have to get at the following: Is there trust? Is there belief in each other's moral and ethical compass? Are our beliefs set in the same core values? If the answers are yes, they can return to a productive working situation knowing that our decision was principled. If it's principled, we know that we can move on. If it's not principled, we may not be able to recover.

—Elementary School Educator

In some districts, adversarial union representation has created a philosophy of disconnection between principal and staff: an "Us-Them" Attitude. People in individualistic cultures tend to blame an individual for problems rather than exploring the broader context in which these problems occur. As a result, the Us-Them Attitude can often target principals and promote a belief that they are ultimately responsible for the dissatisfaction and frustration. Although this is occasionally the case when principals are experienced as micromanaging or as making too many decisions on their own, in reality most principals are also paralyzed in the very same oppressive system. Principals are overworked, isolated, have a limited support system, and rarely any job protection. Yet that is often invisible to staff members.

Sadly, in these situations, everyone loses. Many principals want to collaborate with their staff to minimize workloads. At its worst, the Us-Them attitude divides educators between those who focus on education and children's well-being and those who spend a lot of energy criticizing principals and programs. It polarizes the staff between those who are Pro-principal and Anti-principal, which leads to a very distorted view of who the principal actually is as a person. This process can once again create a vicious cycle where the staff distrusts principals, who are constantly walking on eggshells and defending themselves.

I've developed collaboration with my staff, but, given what's going on in the district, I feel I'm constantly walking on eggs. So far, I am proud to say that I am grievance free, and I really hope it can stay that way.

—Middle School Principal

Sadly, the Us-Them Attitude recruits educators into investing time and energy in conflicts and suspicions instead of focusing on exciting educational practices and professional growth. Ironically, this can require more work, time, and energy than simply compromising on the original issue.

It would be so easy if people could be a little more rational. If we could look at it and say, "This is where you are and this is where they are. There's no way you are going to settle, so why don't you just meet in the middle, instead of sitting there and throwing ugly words at each other for the next three months?"

—First Grade Teacher and Union Representative

RESENTMENT AND NEGATIVITY

We have visited several schools where some educators struggled with Resentment and Negativity. Often, these educators had once given much of their time and energy to their profession and had become unhappy with the constant pressures to do too much and the large number of responsibilities. As a result, Resentment now pushed these teachers away from their preferred selves and would typically get them, for example, to make sarcastic remarks, roll their eyes, or comment negatively in response to others' suggestions. Occasionally, a new teacher struggled with Resentment and Negativity, but most of the time this unhappiness afflicted veteran teachers who had experienced burnout in the profession.

I'm very discouraged now. When I was younger, I didn't understand what the older teachers were complaining about! I had a million other things I wanted to do. I thought [abiding by the contract] was stupid. It seemed fine to me. I can say in hindsight that gradually teachers are doing more and more and more and more for free. They are not valued, not respected, not paid. I think you need to build that awareness in the teachers themselves. The truth is, when you get older you get responsibilities, and then you come to realize how your rights had been eroded.

—Third Grade Teacher

Let us insist on the fact that not all veteran teachers struggle with Resentment and Negativity and, again, that when they are, it is usually as a result of the broader and subcultural pressures they've experienced over many years. Resentment and Negativity clearly don't fit with anyone's preferred self. In fact, the presence of veteran teachers in many schools had a variety of constructive implications. In the new era of increased workload, veterans often become spokespersons for protecting the rights of teachers. They have historical experience with which they can compare current work demands to expectations of five, 10, or 20 years ago. They have lived and witnessed the horrendous increase in the curriculum and responsibility of the teacher. A teacher shared with us that 30 years ago he used to have dinner with students' families and spend more time being involved in arts and afterschool activities with his students. In the past 30 years he has seen the curriculum for fifth grade doubled with no material being removed from it. He speaks:

There is a lot more filling out of forms, more red tape than ever. You have to track the students all year with assessments. We didn't have all of this documentation when I first started. Each season something is being added on and nothing is being taken away. The curriculum is getting bigger and bigger and nothing is being taken away. It does take away from the joy of teaching.

Teachers with such extensive experience can often speak out for the rest of the staff. They know the new demands are unreasonable, and their voices are often heard and respected. In fact, younger teachers who may disagree with or resent some of the administration's demands may not feel that they have the power to speak up and will often count on veterans to do so.

Of course, not all veterans speak out or do so in a public manner. Some veterans may be rather quiet and may prefer one-on-one private communications. Others may be more involved in the mentoring of new teachers rather than being political participants.

Glen Kamoto was a powerful force on campus. He led by example. The legacy of the number of people he's made better will live forever. He would spend hours giving you things, explaining and doing anything for you, but, maybe because of his [heritage], he wouldn't speak up in staff meetings or tell you what to do. He was a role model by his generosity and who he was. I feel honored to have known him.

—Middle School Principal

The distinction between the strong voice that protects and represents teachers' rights versus the one that is experienced as Negative and Resentful lies in the effect it has on others. Resentment and Negativity became a problem in certain schools when their main effects were to undermine others. In those situations, the majority of teachers felt oppressed by the Resentment in the following two ways:

The first problem occurred when Negativity was expressed directly to others as criticism and judgments of their opinions. In those situations staff gatherings became unsafe and less productive. Many teachers in those schools shared how they refrained from contributing creative ideas or expressing their opinions for fear of receiving a sarcastic comment. As one teacher explained, "I wish some teachers thought before they spoke at staff meeting. Everyone should feel safe to share an idea without getting 'shot down' abruptly." This also created a culture of disconnection and distrust. An impoverishment of staff discussions ensued, with a narrowing down of ideas and possible solutions.

The second problem surfaced when the Negativity led to protests against any new or creative attempts to improve or modify traditional practices. A teacher in just such a school shared this with us:

We have a couple of teachers who talk about what they do, without a give-and-take attitude, and who always imply that their way is the only way. It really upsets me and undercuts my own ideas.

In those schools, a significant majority of the staff as well as the principals had become resentful because of the limitations imposed by the Negativity-afflicted teachers, but no actions could be taken because of political seniority and threats of union involvement.

In the schools with those two particular problems, the staff had become completely divided by Negativity and Cliques. In one school, Negativity and Cliques were so powerful that they had some teachers believing that the right to speak came only with experience, and, according to our surveys, new teachers were given surprisingly harsh advice:

Do You Have Advice for New Teachers?

- "Keep your mouth shut and listen to the old-timers"
- "No one wants to hear from a person right out of college who thinks they know it all"
- "Get to know the old-timers and discover why they believe the way they do"
- "Listen and respect experienced teachers—even if they 'know it all'"
- "Don't come off as having all the ideas and don't be too forward"
- "Remember the teachers have been here a while and are used to the way things are"

On average, 32% gave that advice directly. This school had a very small but powerful handful of experienced teachers afflicted with vocal Negativity. It was saddening to see the impression a few people had made on the whole staff. We were left pondering several questions: What is it that keeps certain experienced teachers enthusiastic about their work despite the pressure of specifications and the oppression of the system? How can veterans be honored and appreciated for their experience without putting down the excitement of new teachers? How can schools prevent new teachers' enthusiasm and creativity from being transformed into Negativity after surviving the challenges of the system and its unrealistic pressures? Once Negativity is present, how can a community regroup and reclaim a sense of cohesiveness and excitement for their schools? (See Chapters 4, 5, and 6 for the prevention and resolution of issues similar to these problems.)

COMMUNITY DISRESPECT

Many educators we have spoken to feel quite bitter about the disrespect they have experienced from the community and found it difficult to understand, given the amount of work and care they give in general. A broader analysis of the situation may reveal several factors that can contribute to Community Disrespect. First, when problems arise in schools, the media are very quick to blame and scrutinize teachers. Teachers are visible as workers and stand at the front of the line. Their lower status in the structure of schools and their vulnerability make them easy to blame. Teachers lack the authority that was historically granted by the church and is contemporarily granted by income. Unfortunately, the less authority to validate your voice, the less respect is granted.

Second, in our current time, causality of problems is often simplified and linked to the actions of single individuals. In the fast pace of our lives, it is often tempting to forget that multiple factors contribute to problems and that it is easy to blame whoever is present at the time of the problem.

This simplified perspective can often blame bystanders or people who experienced limited power over a situation.

Third, given that most people have spent a great deal of time in schools, everyone has experiences and ideas about how schools should and shouldn't be. Based on their school attendance as young people, some parents (or reporters) with little knowledge of the actual context may nevertheless feel entitled to make judgments about school programs and personnel. This may lead to educators feeling disrespected because this makes their intentions, efforts, and the complexity of the situation invisible.

Finally, given the unrealistically high expectations and demands placed on teachers, they can only fail, at least in one area. Teachers would have to be superhuman to address all the students' needs, the curriculum, the committee meetings, and balance their own personal lives. Given that teachers cannot succeed with all the pressures placed on them, they are always vulnerable to disrespect, especially from an observer who is unaware of the bigger picture of a teacher's life.

In sum, then, Community Disrespect can be understood as arising from society's general dissatisfaction with the current public educational system and from a problem story of teachers. When teachers feel misrepresented by the media and put down by certain parents (under the influence of this problem story), they become resentful and frustrated toward their profession and sometimes try even harder to fulfill the impossible pressures discuss in Chapter 1. Community Disrespect can unfortunately get teachers to do more to prove their expertise, become more drained from over giving, and, in some situations, develop antagonistic attitudes toward parents.

Interestingly, this problem is less common in many underprivileged and multiethnic communities where families are often grateful for educators' assistance and are less influenced by a problem story.

I am happy to say that I have always felt extremely respected from my school's community. We (my husband and I) teach in a very ethnically diverse community that includes many immigrant families and many lower-income families. We have found them to be extremely supportive—I have gotten no complaints or negativity from my students' families, and they have always demonstrated being extremely grateful for the work I do. The disrespect that I have really been feeling is the lack of respect from the government and the public at large.

—First Grade Teacher

One reason for this can be that in many countries of the world, teachers are regarded with respect as the wise and educated ones in the community. This seems particularly true of cultures less dominated by capitalism (where financial gain in general and "scoring" in the workplace determine your status).

THE RUSHED FEELING AND SCARCITY OF TIME

John Merrow discusses in his book *Choosing Excellence* that teachers are feeling "rushed, crunched and isolated." Educators report that they are constantly running on borrowed time. The Rushed Feeling is a problem that pushes people to act based on speed as opposed to based on their values or better judgment.

A teacher who knew our interest in this subject once volunteered to give us a list of all of the activities she completed in one school day, in addition to the time spent teaching. She was amazed, herself, at the number of things she had to accomplish in a day, not to mention what she accomplished in a 20-minute slot of time (recess) that was supposed to be a "break." Most teachers, despite being well aware of how hard they do work, may be amazed to see a list of all the things they accomplish before school, during breaks, and after school. Statistics have shown that the actual completion of all the school standards would require thousands of additional hours.

Although it would require approximately 15,000 hours to cover the standards and benchmarks currently set forth, there are only 9,000 hours of instruction time available from kindergarten through grade 12. (Marzano & Kendall, 1998)

Many factors contribute to the Rushed Feeling:

- Unrealistic curriculum
- Large number of students
- Little support
- Great needs of families
- Diversity of the job with a great variety of requirements
- High expectations from administration and community
- Excessive amount of responsibility placed on one person

As discussed in Chapter 1 of this book, the messages are "Do more, more, more," "Do little extras constantly," and "It's never enough."

One morning I had a maintenance worker having a heart attack in the parking lot, fire trucks here, and a middle school was visiting with a presentation for the fifth graders. I ended the school day with the afterschool care group giving me a gun that one of the kids had passed to another kid on campus. I then had to deal with a police report, and, finally, the district office wanted me to come to a planning meeting for next year . . .

—Elementary School Principal

The Rushed Feeling is not without costs. It gets teachers and principals to sacrifice their own needs; experience guilt, frustration, and resentment; and be drained of energy to the point of facing professional burnout. As discussed earlier, this kind of stress contributes to a high teacher dropout rate of 30% during the first five years of teaching (Merrow, 2001).

The Rushed Feeling also can reduce the quality of education students are receiving. Learning is reduced to its measured outcome, such as standardized test scores. In the process, many important lessons of life are overlooked and relationships remain superficial, as illustrated in the following story.

> *I was on yard duty. I observed a child leaving her food wrapper on the ground as she left the bench to play. I stopped her and asked her to pick it up and then to pick up ten more pieces of litter because of her negligence. This interaction took less than two minutes and took no real compassion on my part. Later in the day, as I thought about how she walked away sadly, I realized my problem: I am at such a loss for time as a teacher, I feel like I have no time to discuss whether the child would prefer a clean yard over a messy one.*
>
> —Fourth Grade Teacher

This story also illustrates an effect on school culture: Educators under the influence of the Rushed Feeling are using time-efficient ways to solve problems. They attempt to control problems quickly, even if they would prefer facilitating a discussion with children and solving problems more democratically. What often seems to be a quick response to a problem may backfire. In a context where issues cannot be processed and discussed, the common adult decision of punishing, removing an object, or banning a game does not solve a problem, it creates another one. Ultimately, children will not learn to reflect on their actions or how to relate differently and will continue to engage in the behavior in other areas. What is thought to be the most efficient is in the long run less efficient and can contribute further to the Rushed Feeling and teachers having to deal repetitively with similar issues.

Finally, the Rushed Feeling may also get teachers to fall into a survival mode where they are just trying to get things done and keep their heads above water. It can decrease the likelihood of teachers being excited and interested in others' educational successes.

HIERARCHY

Schools are typically organized in a hierarchical fashion, where one person, the principal, governs a group of staff. In turn, teachers are expected to have control over students. Of course, this particular hierarchy is embedded in a much larger one, where the principal reports to the district office, which, in turn, reports to the county and state.

One of the reasons for maintaining this hierarchy is that it is assumed to be more efficient. From a capitalistic perspective, work is more efficient when each worker has a specialized role and the decision-making process is in the hands of only a few. It is certainly faster for one person to make a decision and impose it on others than to take the time to gather input from a group and come to a consensus. Yet we can wonder about the quality and relevance of the decisions made by distant authority figures, as well as people's actual commitment to follow these decisions.

Superintendents have the power to set the tone of staff relationships throughout the district. In our interviews, they reported working hard to develop a context of trust, respect, and democratic exchanges. Despite most superintendents' best intentions, we have come across principals in certain districts who felt the principal's voice would not be heard at the district level.

When principals lead mainly in a hierarchical way, they risk becoming disconnected from the realities of their teachers, making unreasonable decisions, and losing the cooperation, trust, and respect of their staff.

The principal in our school made a big mistake: he asked nonchalantly about everyone's opinion about something, then proceeded to do whatever he wanted without regard for what was expressed. People never forgave him . . . it's ugly sometimes.

—Middle School Teacher

Finally, hierarchy can also lead to responsibilities being shared unequally and ineffectively. In hierarchical situations, people can easily fall into the trap of always expecting the leader to solve problems as opposed to themselves (as mentioned in Chapter 1). A good example of this problem is in teachers' referral of students to the office when a problem arises in the classroom or on the playground. Unfortunately, principals are often removed from situations and may have less information, tools, time, and flexibility of options to solve these problems in the best manner. Teachers develop the habit of simply referring students to a higher level of authority rather than working out the situation, which leads to principals becoming stuck in an endless disciplinary role and teachers losing the respect of students (solutions to this example will be discussed in Chapter 5).

Of course, at times administrators need to make decisions and be accountable for them. It is a difficult balance to maintain, and people in power should never lose sight of the following questions:

If you have power and authority, does that mean you should use it? How do *you* think administrators should draw the line between decisions made in a unilateral way and decisions made in a democratic way? Can you think of decisions made in your school where it was helpful or unhelpful to involve the staff? What was the difference between the two situations? How can administrators ensure that everyone's voice is heard and valued?

COMPETITION

Competition in and of itself is not a bad stance. Its extreme presence in all aspects of education, however, is questionable, as well as the ways in which it is promoted and what is left out. Competition is a cornerstone of capitalism. The assumption is that Competition will increase motivation and performance and will generate the best possible outcome. Although Competition may sometimes have these results, it is not without cost. Competition honors one "winner" and makes the large number of "losers" invisible. From this perspective, then, the number of negative effects can significantly outweigh the positive effects on one "winner." Competition can get teachers to experience resentment, jealousy, discouragement, a sense of inadequacy, and working in isolation with their own ideas as opposed to collaborating. Competition certainly stifles the creativity and sharing that comes with genuine collaboration. When competition dominates a community, it can easily become a problem. This is particularly true in three situations:

- If Competition gets individuals to greatly desire winning or obtaining recognition—in other words, if the prize is highly desirable and the end justifies the mean;
- If Competition is the only or most obvious process by which one can receive appreciation or recognition;
- If individuals are vulnerable to Competition either because of evaluation, self-doubt, overgiving, under-receiving, or a dissatisfying situation.

The following are three of many situations that promote Competition among teachers.

First is the "Teacher of the Year" award, where one teacher gains public appreciation and may get a free dinner. Some teachers greatly appreciate that opportunity and thoroughly understand why one of their colleagues was chosen. Many others, however, wonder how this happened (most teachers work so devotedly). Given that one person wins and countless others don't, we can argue that this process doesn't have the intended effect of promoting appreciation or motivation. In many ways, we can question the validity of the process, its relevance and meaning. In our research, it became clear that most teachers do not begin the school year by stating, "I will work hard this year to get the Teacher of the Year award." Most teachers work hard for other reasons. Near the end of the year, they are asked to evaluate each other's performance and make recommendations for this honor without necessarily being aware of the scope of their colleagues' efforts, achievements, and even how appreciated they are by the students.

Teaching occurs behind closed doors. Some teachers are heroes, others are dangerous. The disparity in skill between teachers within the same district, school, department (etc.) is staggering. I was a very good teacher. Not great, but very good. I also had moments where I was a bad teacher. It is hard to be a fantastic teacher day after day. Some of my colleagues were phenomenal teachers—mentors to me and heroes to the students. I rejoiced when they received public recognition. During my six years of teaching, all teachers who received public recognition for their talent deserved it (and more). My district didn't use the term "teacher of the year." In fact we had no internal competition. Great teachers became "mentor teachers." No one could deny that these individuals were extremely talented. Awards for amazing skill in teaching came from outside the district; I imagine this helped in terms of potential jealousy. Personally, if teachers stand out as particularly skillful and talented I am delighted to celebrate with them in their public recognition. However, "teacher of the year" is a bad term because it is competitive and exclusive.

—Elementary School Teacher

"Bar Raising" is another example of a problem that is subtly invading teachers' relationships with each other. It occurs when teachers who feel dedicated and committed to teaching have decided that they are willing to take on extra responsibilities for the benefit of the school. Other teachers are not willing to do this for personal reasons or because of investment in other areas. The process of Bar Raising inadvertently indicates to the administration that extra work can be completed without compensation. Unless used with caution, these added activities could soon become part of the norm at the school or district level. Bar Raising can also occur with the hiring of new teachers who may be unaware of the historical work expectations at a school site. They may either be influenced by the administration to do more or may find themselves matching the level of performance of Bar-Raising teachers.

I'm pretty new to this school, and, to be honest, worried about myself and my career. There's a bunch of teachers here who work so many extra hours overtime on committees and such without compensation. They are definitely on the career track. I work hard too and love my job, but I have outside commitments that fulfill me, like my dance classes, my volunteer positions, and trying to start a family. I am worried that, compared to them, my commitment level and reputation is going to pale in comparison.

—Second Grade Teacher

The third example pertains to standardized testing. In certain schools, Competition pits teachers against each other, even if it goes against their preferences and personal values.

The thing I think that is not good [about standardized testing] is that I really found myself wanting to know how all the other teachers at my grade level did compared to me. I start to get into "I did this and that, they did this and that." We knew how we did as a grade level and I knew how my class did, but I found myself wanting to know, "Did I do better than (Sandy)? Did (Mary) do better than I?" How awful! I think that's unhealthy to be competitive like that.

—Fifth Grade Teacher

These three situations are simply examples and do not constitute an exhaustive list of the ways in which Competition insidiously affects teachers' relationships. Competition can also recruit teachers to compete for principal attention, parental respect, career gains, student appreciation, status, and popularity, among other things. Competition can get a whole staff to compete with other schools for district approval, grants, status, popularity, and student enrollment. Competition renders visible only that which is the focus of the competition. In that process many other important issues can become overlooked. For example, at a glance, Competition can give a bad impression of the lowest performing or lowest socioeconomic school in the area. The school can even be perceived as the black sheep of the district. Yet, who is to say that the work of educators assisting poverty-stricken, malnourished students to achieve C's is less worthy of recognition than the work of educators who help privileged students to maintain A's? When broader contextual perspectives are taken into account, comparison of and competition between performances often become nonsense.

How can these problems be addressed?

In the next chapters we will explore how to solve these issues once they are undermining a staff, how to invite staff to change these habits in constructive ways, and how to create contexts that will prevent the development of these problems.

NOTES

1. Problems are named and described based on the experiences of the educators in the research and not necessarily based on the best possible externalization.

2. A dual-role relationship refers to a situation where a person's roles may have conflicting demands. For example we have witnessed situations where teachers' union representatives had conflicts with the principal of their schools. Their personal relationship with their principal, as teachers, prevented an objective and neutral role of negotiator with their colleagues' dilemmas.

CHAPTER FOUR

When Serious Problems Divide the Staff

S chool culture issues involving a dominant problem story about principals are always serious since no one then has the leadership or respect of others to facilitate a problem-solving process. Changing such a school environment is certainly not an easy or simple task. Following the narrative approach, one must first gather the participation of all the staff, or, at the minimum, a great majority of the staff. People may not agree on many specific issues and may have developed serious antagonistic relationships, but everyone may agree that the climate is painful and that something has to be done.

If the group can be moved away from its focus on specific individuals to focusing on a joint problem, then a lot can be accomplished. In many schools this requires the involvement of a neutral third party who can act as a professional mediator, gather the trust and respect of everyone, and explore possible territories of resolution. If the budget allows enough time for this mediator, individual meetings with each staff member can be very useful; otherwise a carefully crafted questionnaire may provide the minimum information necessary.

Problems cannot be swept under a carpet and expected to disappear. An anonymous educator shared with us that her principal was not a "touchy, feely kind of a person" and had consequently avoided needed processing sessions with the staff. Over the years, this resulted in an ever-increasing disintegration of the staff and the departure of committed teachers. Any unaddressed issue will undermine the whole culture of the school, teachers' job satisfaction, educational improvement, and, in the end, will result in the most enthusiastic staff leaving.

For this reason we will explore in more depth the development of severely divisive staff problems and ideas to address them.

THE SCENARIO

Elaine Schaffer is the new principal at Jefferson Elementary School. She is taking the place of a much-appreciated colleague who is retiring after a 15-year principalship at Jefferson. Elaine is enthusiastic, committed, and thoughtful. She has been generally well received by the staff, which is mostly pleased with her efforts to get to know them and the families that Jefferson serves. Elaine is quite busy but feels proud of doing things well. She has built connections, promoted academic growth, and observed the running of the school to better understand how Jefferson Elementary ticks. She is known for being everything to everyone at all times. Elaine's first year is celebrated as a success by the district office and the community. She has developed confidence in her abilities to lead the school community, and the district notices that she has done everything by the book.

The second year, Elaine returns with her big heart and her usual enthusiasm. Because of her commitment to education, she has spent the summer reading and attending conferences. She has been exposed to the value of community-building curriculum, mixed-age classes, and cross-age activities. She is considering moving the school in the direction of this philosophy and would like the opinion of the staff. At the first staff development day, everyone arrives filled with the excitement of a new school year. Teachers are filled with the buzz of starting fresh, getting their rooms ready, and being reunited with colleagues. Elaine hands out material to read about multiage classes, student-led conferences, and community meetings. She announces her interest in improving the school's educational stance and her desire for the school to catch up with the latest developments in education. She understands that the staff are quite busy so she requests that they review the material and be ready to discuss it at the staff meeting in two weeks.

After placing a gentle reminder to review the materials in each staff member's mailbox, Elaine is visited by Terry, the most outspoken teacher on the staff. Elaine welcomes her and is surprised by Terry's objections to both the reading assignment and the consideration of a major philosophical change on campus. Terry states, "Why fix something that isn't broken? We are all happy with how things are here." Elaine's response is, "It seems to me that everyone in this school wants to provide the best possible education for our students. I hear your concern, but let's just wait and give the staff a chance to discuss it."

As soon as the meeting is over, Terry walks to Room 15, where she knows many of her grade-level team are congregated. She grumbles to her colleagues about her meeting with Elaine, whom she feels doesn't understand, and how she is mad that Elaine is asking so much in the beginning of the year. Some teachers respond, agreeing that it does sound like a lot for a principal to ask, to read pages of information while they are busy beginning the year, assessing new students, and planning their year. Two other teachers quietly state that they are somewhat intrigued by the changes that could be possible with this new philosophy and while it is a lot of work, they are willing to give it a try.

A week later, Elaine gathers the staff to discuss the reading. She soon discovers a group that is interested in implementing change, a smaller group that is vocally against it with loud Negative voices, and a group that remains silent. After some discussion, Elaine makes an announcement: "Since the majority of those who have voiced an opinion are interested in these ideas and since this is heavily supported by research, let's go forward and give it a try."

In the subsequent weeks, gossip and cliques slowly develop. The staff becomes divided. The union representative schedules a lunchtime meeting to discuss the contract as it applies to the planned changes. As Elaine is becoming increasingly aware that some staff members are rejecting her leadership, she receives a phone call from the superintendent, who is concerned about developments he has overheard about her school.

In response to this situation, Elaine becomes visibly worried. As a result, she becomes more rigid, controlling, and edgy with both teachers and students. Several months later, as things are getting worse and worse, she realizes that she needs assistance and she calls you. How would you go about helping Elaine revitalize her school culture?

APPLYING A NARRATIVE METAPHOR

There could be many ways of addressing the problems faced by the staff at Jefferson School. However, if you intended using the narrative metaphor presented in this book, you would:

1. Find ways of understanding the experience of every-one involved

2. Externalize the problems that accurately represent the experience of each party and map their effects

3. Conceptualize a problematic pattern of interaction

4. Restory and bring forth preferred ways of being for everyone

Understand the Experience of Everyone Involved

Individual staff members need to feel heard, understood, and that their opinion is important. As discussed earlier, individuals' experiences could be gathered either by hiring a neutral third party to briefly interview each person, or, given that cost is often an issue, by giving out a carefully crafted survey.

In this particular context, examples of useful narrative questions are:

- How would you characterize your current school culture? Would you call it a climate of Tension, Distrust, Antagonism, or _____?
- How have you personally been affected by this climate? What does it get you to do, think, and feel that is different from your usual self?
- What have you personally tried to change this problem?
- What do you end up doing to shelter yourself from this problem?
- How has it affected your relationship with your administrator(s)? With your colleagues?
- What are the losses that you currently experience and foresee for the future if this is not addressed?
- Would you be willing to contribute to a movement of improvement? What is the most important reason (for you personally) to change this climate?
- If you were to put aside the laws of budget and reality, would you have any ideas about what could be done?
- What does change mean to you as an educator?

A more thorough and specific survey of the unique situation of the consulting school should be carefully created. All involved should provide information, including administrators and counselors, in an anonymous and confidential way. Once the results are compiled, the staff can be invited into a series of discussions of the results and their implications, with brief handouts being provided as integrated summaries to foster reflection.

Externalize the Problems

Computing the percentages of people experiencing similar negative effects can offer several benefits. First, it moves staff members from a place of alienation and isolation to one of a *shared* experience of discontent. If everyone is unhappy about

Criticism, for example, then everyone can be mobilized to take a stance against It (as opposed to against each other). As slight as this might seem, this shared experience provides a common ground for mobilizing change. Second, an increased awareness of the problem and its effects as well as a clearly articulated conceptualization of the externalized problem can often move the group to another level of processing. If the problem becomes externalized, then participants shift from a position of attacking, defending, or avoiding to one of greater reflexivity and openness to exploration. Third, the new, externalized definition of the problem creates a much larger space for solutions. When people are divided against each other, the focus often becomes which party will succeed at defeating or marginalizing the other. The new perspective offers a much greater number of options for coexistence. In the end, two people may still dislike each other but will perhaps be able to function better and, at the very least, have less of a negative impact on the whole staff.

In our scenario at Jefferson, a survey of the staff revealed that the biggest common problem discussed by most of the staff was the negative and divisive climate dominating their staff. By the time assistance was sought, the issue of change versus no change had almost become secondary. The division rendered everyone distrustful in general. A meeting was scheduled to talk specifically and openly about Distrust (externalization) and its effects on everyone. Given the nature of the problem and its silencing effect, the early phases of this process had to be facilitated with patience and compassion. Several staff members courageously began to share their grief and longing for lightheartedness and more collaboration. The staff was asked what Distrust had taken away from their school. Many commented on the absence of spirit and enthusiasm, the dwindling of collaboration and mentorship, fewer social gatherings, and less commitment. One teacher commented shyly that the most obvious indicator of the staff's mood was the absence of chocolates and other treats in the staff room. She reminded others of the former state of the staff room where people talked, laughed, shared, and ate sweets together. When asked where Distrust was leading the school, many thought they were heading for burnout and frankly were looking for other job opportunities. They were also worried about the reputation of their school. In the end, most candidly acknowledged that Distrust had the following important effects:

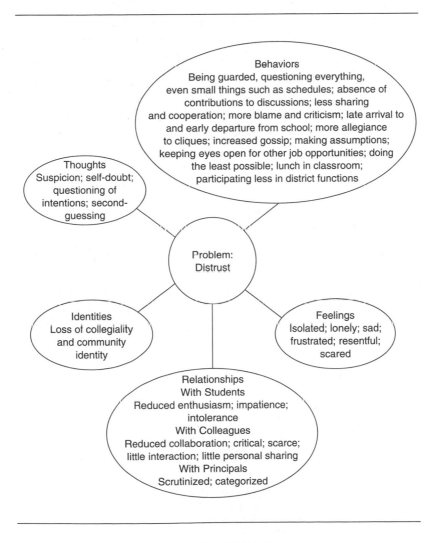

Conceptualize a Pattern of Interaction

You may be wondering . . . how did Elaine respond to these developments? While Distrust had all the effects discussed above on the staff, it also had effects on the principal. In response to the problem situation, Elaine became increasingly defensive. She had always dreamed of being a leader who earned respect rather than demanded it, and she grieved the loss of that identity. She found herself being less collaborative and more secretive about decisions than she preferred, but felt she had no choice. She was losing sleep and gaining weight. She found herself dressing in more conventional suits to assert her professional status and disprove the reputation of her being an unrealistic idealist. She felt trapped and isolated in her role. In an attempt to reduce her isolation she developed closer relationships with certain staff members, which also gave her a reputation of playing favorites.

In the end, Defensiveness pushed Elaine away from her preferred self and into the following ways of being:

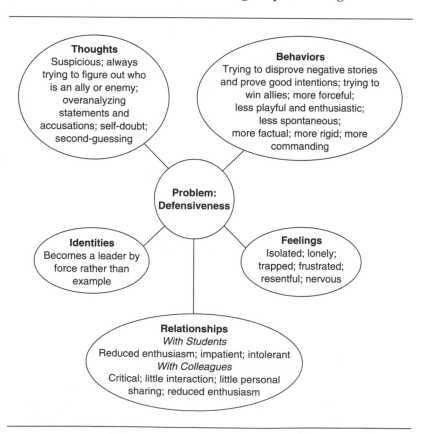

The more Elaine was under the influence of Defensiveness, the more the staff became distrustful, disconnected, and unresponsive. Elaine started perceiving the staff as unwilling, negative, and uncooperative, while the staff developed a story of Elaine as being forceful and smug. In this process, everyone started noticing little behaviors that confirmed each of their problem-saturated stories.

The only way vicious cycles of interactions can be broken is when both parties become keenly aware of their contributions to the pattern and very articulate about how the externalized problem pushes them into acting against their better judgment (their preferred versions of themselves). Everyone was invited to notice for themselves times when Distrust or Defensiveness might infiltrate their brain and influence their decision to engage or not to engage in a certain way of being.

As everyone became more articulate and increasingly aware of each moment in the day when they were making decisions based on Distrust or Defensiveness rather than on their preferred self, they began to gain a little more power over their own contribution to the climate. The facilitator eventually engaged the staff in the sharing and discussion of the times when they could have chosen to operate under the influence of Distrust or the problem stories, but instead consciously chose not to. While this exercise was challenging early on, people progressively noticed that they had actually sheltered some interactions from Distrust or problem inter actions. In other words, Distrust or Defensiveness was not necessarily there 100% of the time. Even though it was there a lot of the time, some small instances of collaboration and connection were still cherished. One teacher, Juliet, shared her happiness at still being able to meet with two colleagues for planning meetings that she said were lighthearted, friendly, and completely cooperative. The facilitator became intrigued by Juliet's experiences and attempted to articulate and bring forth the ingredients of those preferred interactions. Juliet pondered for a moment and then shared how they had formed a friendship based on sharing and connecting ever since bonding on a long bus ride home after a field trip. She continued that she knew for a fact that these colleagues had very similar educational philosophies and shared common goals.

Although it is commonly useful to invite a staff to explore their joint philosophy as a group, it is always preferable to have the usefulness of this activity presented by the staff themselves, rather than having it forced upon them by a facilitator or a leader, especially given the history of the problem.

The staff was then asked what effect it would have on Distrust if their goals and philosophies were made visible. As most people recognized that knowledge about others would probably assist in reducing Distrust, another meeting was scheduled to try to explore each other's vision as educators. In our experience, staff that have had the opportunity to discuss, explore, and articulate a common vision that is truly inclusive of everyone's ideas is the best starting place in any transition. In the end, most educators will agree that they want what is best for kids even if the ways in which this is done can include some nuances (see the last section of this chapter for more).

This meeting proved to be very fruitful as it became visible that despite Cliques, Distrust, and Negativity, most valued their relationship with students, quality education, school as a community, and personal growth. However, they were clear that they didn't want growth to be forced, as they already felt overextended and needed time to read and think about newly presented ideas. Distrust had created a context in which they feared being forced toward change. They hadn't taken the time to explore whether or not they would welcome change. In other words, when anticipating force, most people automatically prepare to counter that force. The process always takes precedence over consideration of the nature of change.

Making Visible Intentions, Values, and Preferred Identities

The discussion of the staff's vision was followed by an invitation to make visible the principal's vision and leadership dreams. This can be done effectively by interviewing the principal in front of the whole staff. For this to be meaningful, principals have to trust their interviewers and feel confident that the conversation will make visible their preferred ways of being. The interview can assist both the principal and the staff to realize that the intentions were originally compassionate and well meaning, even though the method and effects may have been overly negative.

With that in mind, Elaine was interviewed and asked the following questions:

- What were your hopes and dreams when you decided to become an educator?
- Was there an educator who was particularly inspiring to you? What was it about this person that you admired?
- What was it like for you as a teacher? What is your fondest memory? What was your biggest struggle?
- What was your vision when you decided to be an administrator?
- What are you proud of having accomplished with your staff at your previous school?
- What did you most appreciate about this staff at Jefferson when you first arrived?
- Is there a particular moment that you remember experiencing with this staff that made you think highly of them?
- I know from our personal conversations that you are committed to respecting your staff and leading in a democratic way. Even though it may not always have worked that way, what were your intentions in balancing your role as an administrator with the desires of your staff? Do you recall an instance where you were able to put thought into making it happen?
- The staff have discussed that Change means a lot of work for them. What does Change mean to you?
- The staff have commented that Distrust has taken away their sense of community and enthusiasm. What has the Distrust cycle taken away from you?

- You and your staff have been through quite a bit of suffering. What is it that keeps you coming back each day? How is it that you haven't given up on this school?
- Is there anything that I haven't asked you that you would like to make visible at this point? (See Resource B for a more thorough interview.)

After such conversation, everyone is usually more open and receptive to new perceptions (stories) of each other. In this situation, for example, Elaine restoried her perception of the staff from unwilling to interested but hesitant. The staff also restoried their perception of Elaine from forceful and idealistic to seeing her more as a compassionate person. Their view of her included the fact that she was a dedicated leader who became blindsided by her enthusiasm. It became visible to the staff that Elaine's intentions were not to force them into change but rather to invite them into a process. Her enthusiasm and exploration of these ideas, however, had taken place in isolation during a summer vacation, and, without her realizing it, she had moved too quickly beyond the staff's experience.

With Distrust and Defensiveness shrinking and preferred stories of people becoming more visible, the school moved to a phase of teambuilding where connections were fostered beyond superficial characteristics, age, years of experience, and hobbies (Beaudoin & Walden, 1997; Heatherington, 1995).

Eventually a committee was formed to explore the educational advancement of the school. They selected a few educational bestsellers that were made available to interested staff, but otherwise summarized and presented. The staff then freely discussed their interest in pursuing some of these ideas. A few particularly interested teachers volunteered to try some of these ideas, and Elaine supported people's personal pace when experimenting with new concepts in their classrooms. The pioneers were then invited to report back to the staff as to the effects they had noticed on the students and on themselves as educators, as well as the direct feedback they received from the students and their families. As a result, more and more teachers became interested in exploring and experimenting with these concepts, finding ways to make them their own. Elaine, in the end, became the principal she had always wanted to be: supporting her teachers in their own quest for educational enlightenment. The staff ultimately became strengthened by this journey, and they developed a greater empathy for each other, including Elaine, who became included as one of them.

If you ever visit Jefferson Elementary School, you will notice that chocolate and other treats now abound in the staff room!

Can principals bring change in their school's philosophy or practices without going through all these problems?

CHAPTER FIVE

Changing Staff Habits Without Conflict

PROCESS OF CHANGE

Readers must be cautioned against the temptation to implement radical change too quickly in their school environment. It is part of this philosophy to institute change through dialogue and discussions, in a process, rather than imposing it. Change can really only happen if all involved have had a chance to reflect on the process, articulate their personal position on the issues, experiment with the process, and eventually become committed to the idea that it serves their best interests. This process in itself can take anywhere from a few months to a few years, depending on the number of people involved and their level of alignment with it. Adjustments will have to be made along the way. Regardless of the time spent in conversation, the process is more important than the outcome. It is in the process that the values of cooperation, respect, and appreciation are truly expressed. In the end, the lived experience of these ideas will serve as the foundation for building an improved school culture.

If the staff have developed a particularly negative story about a principal, it may be almost impossible for this principal to facilitate conversations that chip away at the problem story. Remember, if a problem story is very elaborate, people will pay attention only to information that confirms the negative perspective.

Implementing a New
Idea or Changing the Status Quo

Novelty is always frightening to some and exciting to others. You can be assured that you will have both extremes represented in a staff. For many, the mere thought of changing a practice that has been relied on for 10 or 20 years can trigger significant amounts of insecurity, doubt, concern over the time required, and reluctance to do what may appear to be extra work. For others, the prospect of experimenting with new ideas and staying up to date with new educational ideas is paramount and a vital source of enthusiasm. Regardless of your personal position, you have to be willing to understand and patiently collaborate with those who hold another position. Remember that people always have a reason to be a certain way; your own willingness to take risk may have developed from a life of safety and/or successful experimentation, while others might have suffered greatly from harsh transitions and instabilities.

Any significant change of philosophy has to occur both from the bottom up and from the top down. The principal can expose the staff to ideas, distribute reading material, invite speakers on the subject, organize visits to other schools that have successfully implemented the idea, and support individual teacher excitement over trying new practices. As discussed in previous chapters, principals have little power, in reality, and cannot require a change without risking sabotage or resentment from reluctant staff. Moreover, if people do not want to engage in a new practice or are not committed to it, it will almost certainly fail, thereby "proving" its inadequacy. As in most situations, collaboration and allowing each person his or her own unique pace of slow or rapid change will, in the end, change the school in a much more efficient way.

Principals commented on this process:

You can't change overnight. I work with those teachers who want to [change] and you build a successful program slowly.

I look for ways to support people that are taking little tiny steps. I work with the people who are in favor of [an innovative new idea] and let their success speak for itself. I would say, "Go ahead. You really believe in this, go ahead!"

—Elementary School Principal

We used to have a student of the month award but it didn't work because I had to constantly press the teachers for the students' names, waste my time going over and over again to the staff when they hadn't thought about it, and often ended up facilitating the event on my own in front of parents and students with the awarding teachers not showing up. We stopped it. If the teachers aren't backing the idea, it just won't work.

—Middle School Principal

Resolving Minor Problems

Problems are minor when they involve a smaller number of individuals, are not related to the principal's perceived integrity, have a limited impact on everyone, happen only occasionally, are of limited intensity, or are recently developed. Problems such as gossip, problem-saturated communication, competition, and the like, can usually be addressed by honest group discussions. The principal or facilitator can engage the staff in a discussion of the effects of this problem or invite grade-level teams to review the matter in smaller, private groups. Ultimately each individual has to come to an understanding of the personal efforts and benefits that would ensue from changes. Another option is to invite speakers with an expertise in the area or representatives from another school who might have successfully implemented the new idea.

STEP-BY-STEP EXAMPLE OF THE THINKING BEHIND A CONSTRUCTIVE PROCESS OF CHANGE

Many principals nowadays want their staff to stop sending students to the office for discipline. They are clear that they didn't join the profession to punish lines of students after recess and feel that it is highly ineffective in developing student-teacher problem solving. Many principals will be tempted to simply tell their staff to stop the referral process. This sometimes works; however, it often doesn't. Consider the following:

If You Can Use Power, Does That Mean That You Should?

Principals certainly have the power to determine new procedures and rules in their school . . . in theory. In our example, imposing this new procedure is likely to anger the staff, particularly those who send students to the office all the time! If some of the staff are angry, there will simply be a switch in problems for principals: Instead of dealing with upset students, they will have to deal with resentful staff. In some case, principals have to deal with a bigger problem because upset teachers generally deal with students in negative ways, especially if the teachers feel powerless.

Do Not Pull the Rug Out From Under People Before They Have Something Else to Stand On

Teachers who constantly send students to the office are also sending the administration a message: They do not know how to handle these situations in an effective manner. Telling them to stop sending students to the principal's office will not necessarily empower them to solve things in a more effective manner. In reality, such a rule may create an experience of powerlessness, fear, and being overwhelmed and, further, bring out the worst in teachers who have no other means of handling the situation. This may at times simply escalate conflicts to such a level that there really is no choice other than sending the student to the office. These teachers, more than anyone else, need time to think and articulate why change is useful in order for them to explore alternative options willingly. Pulling the carpet out from under their feet will focus their attention on resentment against the principal instead of on the development of new problem-solving strategies.

The Farther Away One Is From Better Practices, the Less an Intellectual Presentation Is Likely to Work

Teachers, just like everyone else, will respond to an intellectual presentation[1] on class management or attitude only if it is close to their experience. In other words, teachers who will benefit from these types of workshops are usually those who are already committed to learning such practices or who feel that the presentation adds interesting nuances to their current ideologies. For individuals who most need it, the presentation will slide over their heads like water slides off a duck's back. For many, the presentation and its implications, even though amusing and interesting, may be long forgotten when the busyness of the school year starts.

Questions Are Cost-Effective

Although it may seem more effective time wise to simply tell or present to people what to do, in reality that is likely to end up being much more time-consuming and less effective.[2]

In our example (reducing office referrals), people will not fully grasp why and how they are supposed to deal with this situation, which will leave the administrator not only having to deal with upset staff as discussed above but also having to give advice, which seldom works. In a narrative approach, the savvy administrator will assist the staff in articulating their own concerns about the process of referring students to the office. The starting point is the same as it was initially for the principal, which is that of simply wondering what the effects are of sending students to the office. A principal can either gently invite the staff in a conversation or ask their counselor, a neutral third party, to facilitate the process (especially if the principal is very invested in the outcome). As discussed in Chapter 2, the staff can be engaged in a discussion externalizing "Referrals" and systematically mapping its effects on multiple areas. For example:

- What are the general effects of Referring students to the office?
- Has anyone noticed how this affects your relationship with them? Is your long-term relationship with students improved, unaffected, or worsened by Referrals?
- When Referring is frequent, how do students talk, feel, and think about their teachers? Do students have more respect or less for teachers who refer?
- What does Referring tell students about you as a teacher? Might it inadvertently convey a certain message about your authority or ability to handle situations?
- When students come back to your classroom after being Referred, how do they perform? Are they the same as before, more likely to participate, succeed, and be on task, or to be frustrated and withdrawn?
- How does it affect your day and your teaching to have these conflicts/referrals with students?
- Would you all be willing to experiment with fewer Referrals for the next two weeks and discuss your experience in our next meeting?

Listen to All Voices

Clearly some staff members will be in favor of the status quo and will want to voice their appreciation of existing systems such as Referrals. The process of exploring the effects of school practices, such as Referrals, can certainly include a list of advantages. Ideally, two columns can be drawn on a board with the facilitator writing down the staff's reflections on positive and negative effects. It is important to listen to it all and to leave space for teachers to reflect freely without feeling pressured in any particular direction. Pressure will usually result in counterpressure, leaving little space to ponder and reflect in any meaningful way. Being open to hearing advantages and disadvantages will create a nonjudgmental context that will foster flexibility and trust. This same attitude is crucial to hold when connecting to students.

Principals are becoming increasingly interested in students' voices and are exploring various ways to invite them into the educational system. In doing that, however, some fall in the trap of privileging the newer voices at the expense of the older voices. Silencing teachers and siding with students will typically not solve the problems, but rather shift them elsewhere. Teachers who do not feel heard and respected by their administrators are less likely to respect students. This can create a scenario where students (and their families) complain to the administration, which then tries to manage teachers, who become increasingly resentful at students. A triangle of interaction is never optimal in any situation. If the goal is to provide a respectful environment, then the method must be thoughtfully respectful of all. Decisions are also generally enriched by including the contributions of multiple voices and perspectives.

Listening Is Communicating That You Understand

Whether you are a principal or an educator, listening is probably one of the most important practices you can develop if you truly believe in a community. Listening is a much harder "activity" than everyone thinks for two main reasons:

1. People speak about 125 words per minute in our culture, while our brains can actually process about 800 words per minute (Communication Research Associates, 1995). This means that most people can listen to the content of a speech and, at the same time, in the back of their mind, take mini mental vacations elsewhere, or make negative judgments or large numbers of assumptions. Have you ever experienced the frustration of not feeling listened to by someone and yet, when challenged, the person can actually retell the content of the conversation? The retelling of the content usually doesn't alleviate

the experience of feeling not heard because you know the listening was not of high quality. Quality listening is about using the remaining capacity of your brain to do the following:

- Imagine what it's like to live the particular experienced talked about
- Relate to its implications
- Spend energy understanding how it makes total sense for this person (given their context)
- Put yourself in their shoes
- Ask relevant, empathetic *questions*

Listening is an active process. It is different from hearing, even on the physiological level; you actually spend more calories and have a faster pulse when actively receiving information.

2. Listening is also about letting the other person know that you understand. Again, people will not feel listened to unless you communicate to them that they are heard. This usually requires a stance of compassion, collaboration, curiosity, and genuine interest in the person's experience (as discussed in Chapter 2). For staff members to feel heard, the facilitator or principal must often repeat the statements that were made, or, more specifically, restate what *you* understood, with a genuine attempt to understand and not judge.

Think of Long-Term and Solid Instead of Quick and Upsetting

Although the first two weeks after such discussions may lead to a few more referrals than if a new rule had been established, they will likely be less than the usual routine. Staff may try different ways of managing issues in their classrooms, which at times will be successful and at others quite exhausting. In the process, however, they are thinking and exploring, which is laying a very solid foundation for long-term, successful change.

Change Is a Process, Not an Event

When the staff reconvenes, teachers can be invited to discuss the times they could have Referred but didn't and how they successfully handled those situations. A list of each staff member's unique resolution of the situation can be made on the board. Often people are tentative initially and have not even articulated for themselves how they actually handled the situation differently. It is useful that the facilitator, whether the principal or another, is comfortable asking for the details of what they tried, the effects on students, what it meant to student, how they felt as educators afterwards, and so on. In the meantime, others who may have been less invested in the change are listening and learning lived, meaningful strategies from each other. The process of sharing strategies that have been experienced and successful for a colleague is much more powerful than having a didactic training on management. One is connected with experience, the other with intellectual learning. One will be remembered for the richness and relevance of the story, the other will be forgotten like a chemistry formula. The sharing and exploring creates a powerful process of change to which everyone can become profoundly committed.

Contrast Intentions and Effects (Using Another Example)

I was consulting at a new school. I spent several very pleasant lunches chatting with a few interested teachers about my work. One male teacher in particular was very much in agreement with some of my beliefs around education. He shared how he loved his work as a teacher and believed in creating a safe and exciting context for learning. For that to happen, he said, "You have to let go of unnecessary disciplining and really build a caring connection with your students. Students learn best when they have nothing to worry about except discovery of new material." As the bell rang and everyone went back to their classrooms, I was left alone, pondering on how lucky these children were to have such a kind and devoted teacher.

As I walked back to the office to touch base with the principal, I was suddenly pulled out of my thoughts by screaming sounds. I was getting closer to a classroom where a teacher was yelling at a student: "This is MY classroom, and I can do whatever I want here! You don't deserve to be in MY room! Get OUT NOW and sit outside! I will teach you to be respectful!" A young boy burst out of the class, became embarrassed when he saw me, and collapsed by the door, in tears. As I approached the student, I could see through the window that the teacher was the gentleman I had just left.

Were this teacher's intentions the most accurate representation of who he was? Or was it his behavior? Who would you say is the real person?

Several months later, as complaints and concerns arose about this teacher, the principal asked me if I would get involved in that class. After I respectfully approached the teacher, asked him his understanding of the problem, and connected with him, he became interested in exploring some ideas with me.[3]

From a narrative perspective, this gentleman was gently invited into a conversation about his intentions and the effects that his behaviors actually had. His increased awareness of the incongruence between intentions and effects assisted him in making a decision about who he preferred to be.

At a later time, I gently interviewed him in front of his students about his values and life experiences around respect. The process assisted him further in publicly articulating his goals and preferences, and allowed students to better understand what was personally important for him in terms of respect and why. I was later told by several students and the principal that this teacher had developed a very good connection with his class. The principal was relieved to have fewer complaints about an educator she knew was very committed to his work.

Think Meaning, Not Facts

Facts never stand alone. They are always interpreted and ascribed meaning. People usually interpret and ascribe meaning based on their own personal experience with, inadvertently, very little consideration for the actual context of others' lives. When witnessing or speaking to someone who has engaged in a negative practice, make sure to consider the bigger canvas of this incident, how the person thinks of him- or herself as a person (story), and how he or she believes others interpret the action. Noticed events always carry meaning, and addressing that meaning is of the utmost importance in bringing about any significant change. The gentleman discussed above was eventually engaged in a conversation about the meaning of being respectful to students and what it said about him as an educator.

NOTES

1. An intellectual presentation is one in which the facilitator presents expert concepts and ideas before a mostly passive-listening audience. This can be useful at times but will not lead to any significant climate change in itself. This process is in contrast to the material presented in this book about engaging educators in a discussion, where the facilitator mostly asks questions and invites everyone to reflect and articulate the changes they would like to make and which strategies best suit their unique styles. Another example of this active process is inviting teachers into experiential exercises to increase their awareness of their own behaviors and communication styles. People in general are more likely to learn and change through observing their own limitations in action rather than being told to do something differently. An interactive process empowers them to be committed to change. Examples of such activities can be found in Resource B of this book.

2. This same limitation applies to students. Principals, who often have limited school budgets, may hire volunteers or people with no clinical training to do the counseling work. Although these people may be invaluable in connecting with students and have compassionate intentions, they may end up simply engaging in giving advice, which will assist only the few students with minor issues. A more successful approach is to keep these generous

volunteers as student mentors and hire a trained professional for a few hours per week for the more complex sufferings and problems.

3. I would never impose myself in a classroom or to a teacher at the request of the principal. Teachers must be approached respectfully and involved in choosing whether or not they are interested in exploring the climate in their classroom.

CHAPTER SIX

Preventing Problems and Creating a Climate of Support

I n this chapter we will cover aspects of what we have come to consider as the ingredients of a climate of respect, appreciation, and collaboration. Aside from instances when problems have to be solved, it is important to establish a general climate of belonging that will prevent these problems from developing and minimize conflicts in difficult times.

In our survey regarding job satisfaction, we found that the four strongest predictors of teachers' job satisfaction, in order of importance, were: (1) sharing of materials (collaboration), (2) relationship with principal (personal connection, trust, and approachability), (3) appreciation by colleagues, and (4) general connection with staff (see Figure 6.1). We also found a negative correlation between the experience of disrespect from students and job satisfaction. In other words, the equation that could predict teachers' job satisfaction would read as follows:

Job Satisfaction = Connection + Collaboration + Appreciation + Trusting Relationship With Principal – Disrespect

Figure 6.1   The four strongest predictors of teachers' job
satisfaction

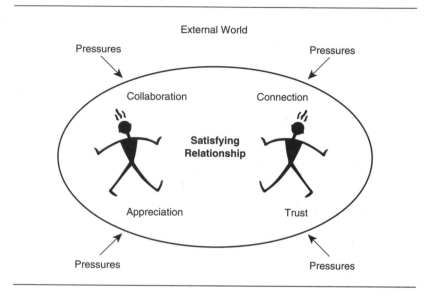

We will present these powerful components as well as others that, although not formally included in our surveys, became obvious in interviews and in our full research.

CONNECTION

Schools are often presented as the ultimate cradle of socialization for children, and teaching is often considered one of the most social professions for adults. Interestingly, however, conversations with adults and children often reveal a profound sense of alienation, isolation, and disconnection that is further intensified by the innumerable possibilities for relationships. In other words, there is nothing worse than feeling alone in a crowd, and that is true for both students and adults.

By connection we mean a process of being open and accepting of the other as a whole person, with his or her multiple versions of self. It is a process of valuing diversity at all levels, including ethnicity, religion, age, generation, interest, experience, and more. In this compassionate process of honoring each other, we find the best is brought out in each individual. Connection is about *being* together, as well as *doing* joint activities.

Connections among staff create a shield against problems and foster a nurturing environment where solutions are easily generated.

For connections to develop in a group, people need to agree that connection is part of the climate they want to create and promote for each other. Principals can certainly set the tone for such a philosophy, as some have done. Ultimately, however, the principal can do only so much. The staff need to be recruited into a joint agreement on the importance that *they* want to ascribe to connections in their school culture.

As discussed in the process of change section in Chapter 5, the staff can be invited to make a list of what it means to have connections. Common, agreed-upon ingredients for meaningful connection include trust, safety, time, attentive presence, nonjudgmental listening, honesty, compassion, perspective, and humor, among others. When you, the reader, think about your current school culture, what is the number of people with whom you experience these characteristics? (See Table 6.1.)

Table 6.1   When you, the reader, think about your current school culture, what is the number of people with whom you experience these characteristics?

Ingredients	Ingredients of Connection That I Value	Number of Colleagues With Whom I Experience This Ingredient
Trust		
Safety		
Time		
Attentive presence		
Nonjudgmental listening		
Honesty		
Compassion		
Perspective		
Humor		
Other		

Developing and maintaining rich connections, as discussed here, might seem to take a lot of time, but it doesn't have to.

Several principals report having staff meetings every other week, mostly to process issues and connect with each other. Dry information can be distributed in staff memos or informally by a small group of elected grade-level representatives instead of being discussed in depth in meetings to make room for more meaningful connections. One of the most basic ways of creating a more harmonious staff climate is to have a discussion on teachers' educational values and philosophies. A certain sense of unity in educational mission and goal can go a long way. This is particularly true about educational philosophies, where educators, committed to a cocreated set of values or a mission statement, may connect on a deeper level.

Connections can be further developed when staff have opportunities to share a wide range of information about themselves. There is a point where people know so much about each other that similarities are easily found, even on school sites where educational philosophies are wide ranging. Sometimes it is simply about making the person behind the role more visible. An example of this would be to publish teachers' biographies along with their values, hobbies, and special interests. Once made available to the community, a teacher's biography would make the multiple aspects of the person behind the role more visible, more human and interesting.

We have facilitated workshops where we engaged participants in a merging stories exercise: Participants co-construct a single story of their lives as if they were one person (see Resource B). Through this process they notice how rich and diverse each person's experience has been, and they deepen their intimacy through the sharing of historically important events in their lives. A version of a similar process was experienced by an elementary school principal:

In a round table "big wig" meeting, the head of the meeting asked everyone to tell their story. He started with his story, which set parameters for the people that followed. This made it safe, so by the time the guts of the meeting started, everyone was equal.

Regardless of title, experience and backgrounds, the playing field was leveled. I will facilitate that exercise in my new school in September.

Connections are invaluable in contributing to teachers' job satisfaction, sense of belonging to their school, and, in the end, to their performance. Deeper connections would solve or at least reduce problems such as gossip, cliques, problem-saturated conversations, and competition. The specific method of connecting is not as important as it happening in a meaningful way. For some it may be a phone conversation, for others it may entail putting paperwork aside and spending time in another's classroom. For still others it may simply be using time already available, such as lunches and recesses, to talk about more energizing and connecting subjects (as opposed to problem-saturated gossip).

You have got to be connected to survive. [My principal] and I talk on the cell phone each evening when we are driving home to process how things are going.

—Middle School Assistant Principal

In our research, it seemed that women principals actively promoted connection in their staff more often than men. Although this could simply be a sampling bias, there is a possibility that women may be more comfortable in promoting social relationships because they benefit from a thorough socializing process of caring and expressing feelings that is not consistently offered to boys (Ashton-Jones, Olson, & Perry, 2000; Kimmel & Messner, 1998; Pollack, 1999; Tannen, 1990). This woman principal, for example, shared a list of examples of practices, while several male principals would mostly refer to parties as the main process to develop relationships:

At each meeting, I try to include some sort of opportunity for sharing personal issues. Sometimes we talk about where we are. I also have these "angel cards," so we each will pull a card and discuss what it means. Other times we draw a face about what we each are feeling right now, and we'll have conversation about that.

Finally, fun times are always an opportunity for people to see each other in a different light and develop deeper connections. Some schools organize nonwork-related, fun, social gatherings. Other schools will reserve a piece of their budget to organize team-building retreats where people play games, engage in personal reflections, and spend time together. Finally others, even from underprivileged schools, reserve funds to send any interested teachers to special and interesting conferences as a group, as illustrated in this example:

If you manage the budget right, you can have resources for conferences. We try to send as many people as we can to this conference. Sometimes up to twenty go. We'll book airfare and hotels for them. They all fly down together and stay together and have a wonderful experience doing that. I have really committed myself to providing them with something special.

—Middle School Principal

On a daily or weekly basis, school staffs could determine ways to structure recesses and lunches so that teachers can spend time connecting with each other instead of having yard duty. When the staff is really committed to connection and develops even the habit of sitting at one big table, these few minutes of time together can be really significant:

Our staff sits together around one big table. Once we had to split our tables for a California State Distinguished School visit, and the staff was so uncomfortable! At the end of that day we shoved the tables together and everyone felt better.

COLLABORATION

In most schools that we visited and/or surveyed, teachers' most frequent comment about each other and the staff was the presence or absence of collaboration. This was also the strongest predictor of job satisfaction on another independent survey. In general, teachers were extraordinarily grateful to their colleagues for sharing ideas, materials, advice, and the workload (see Box 6.1).

Box 6.1

In our research, we found that teachers experienced being a team member, collaborating, and sharing as the top three most helpful aspects of their staff relationships. The following are examples of teachers' comments on what they valued in staff relationships:

1. Being a Team Member

- Sharing ideas, information, strategies, and materials
- Interacting and sharing information about successes they are having
- Planning lessons together as a team
- Offering help; for example, running copies for each other
- Working together on special events

2. Connecting in Friendship and Camaraderie

- Talking with you and being willing to really listen
- Smiling, finding humor in daily situations, laughing together, being cheerful
- Extending themselves with a friendly, inviting attitude
- Being supportive daily, but especially during a crisis
- Showing appreciation

(Continued)

Box 6.1 (Continued)

3. Sharing Professional Encouragement

- Offering encouraging words and emotional support
- Giving reassurance and support in and out of the classroom
- Offering suggestions and giving advice

Significant collaboration can happen only when people are connected. In other words, collaboration occurs within the shadow of connection. Collaboration also occurs at different levels. The extent of the collaboration depends on the school's and the teachers' philosophies. Many schools have a minimum level of collaboration, such as sharing materials within grade levels. Schools that are most collaborative coteach, team-teach, discuss philosophies, exchange classes, and peer-coach, among other practices. In addition to the extent (quantity) of collaboration, there seem to be two main types (quality) of collaboration: horizontal and vertical.

Horizontal collaboration is the close working relationship between colleagues at the same grade level. This is common and very necessary. Practices include grade-level meetings, swapping classes for coverage of different subject matter, and co-teaching.

Vertical collaboration occurs across grade levels and across hierarchies. Its occurrence is infrequent yet equally valuable. It involves teachers working with all ages of students, or teachers of one grade level working with another, or principals switching places with teachers as illustrated in the following stories.

This year I am teaching a sixth grade class and swapping places with a teacher. This teacher is interested in an administrative career and appreciates the opportunity to work in the office, while I enjoy the opportunity to work with the students and build a relationship that will last during their stay at this school. I love teaching this class. It's something really special in my day, and we do all sorts of cool and meaningful projects.

—Middle School Principal

I have lately wondered why we don't collaborate across grades. For example, when I taught about water in second grade, I realized the kids were also studying water at fifth grade. Why didn't we get together and do cross-age projects based on students working together, teaching each other and collaborating?

—Elementary School Teacher

Collaboration offers many advantages. It:

- Reenergizes
- Fosters an open mind and creativity
- Generates a greater number of ideas when faced with a problem
- Fuels enthusiasm and fun
- Provides rewarding experiences of shared success
- Can increase performance (which is not the reason to promote collaboration, but it is a profitable side effect)

I have a colleague who will always share with me. She's not stingy with her ideas at all. I truly feel like she wants me to be successful, and I feel like it was her that made me successful here last year. I was able to get a good name in one year, and that's real hard to do. She introduced the intrinsic rewards, you know, how to look for a little more out of teaching. She said I'm going to take you through it this year, and she really held my hand. You have to have those people.

—Elementary School Teacher

THE MANY FACES OF APPRECIATION

Gratitude is the best medicine for the illnesses of our community life.

—P. Johnson Fenner, 1995

Appreciation, as we define it, is expressing acknowledgment. The intention is to be transparent about our personal experience of gratitude or admiration. Sharing appreciation is a process of the genuine expression of gratefulness without the intention to alter the recipient's behavior in any way. As discussed throughout this book, educators work so hard, give so much of their time, money, and devotedness, that in the end they can be very hungry for appreciation. Yet appreciation is scarce. Everyone recognizes its value and craves it, yet people lack the context and means to express it in meaningful ways. Invisible obstacles can limit the ease with which it is expressed. In a 15-minute break, problem-saturated communication may be perceived as more important than the expression of appreciation; hierarchical relationships may create a unidirectional pattern for the expression of feedback, including appreciation; feeling rushed may get teachers to be task-oriented and therefore forget their preferred value of acknowledgment. In some situations, this absorption into roles may disconnect educators from their own human experiences around connection. People become task oriented, and appreciation becomes a tool rather than an experience.

In most of the schools we have visited, however, it was often astonishing to interview principals who would systematically elaborate on all the ways they attempted to promote appreciation and then to find in our surveys the extent to which the staff actually felt unappreciated. Upon further reflection, the explanation became obvious: One person can have the experience of giving a large amount of appreciation, yet when divided among 30 staff members and a large number of children, the amount each recipient experiences may be minute.

It became clear to us that for a context of appreciation to exist, the distribution of acknowledgment should be circulated by a larger number of people. This means a less hierarchical system needs to exist where appreciation offered by people in lesser positions of power also become meaningful. In other words, appreciation offered by a principal then carries more or less equal weight as appreciation offered by a peer. A good example of this is when teachers pass on a small symbol of appreciation from one to another each month.

Ideal systems allow appreciation for everyone and by everyone. The student population is an enormous pool of appreciation untapped by most schools. Once again, this may be due to the lower status ascribed to students in a hierarchical system. It is particularly surprising given that ultimately most educators went into education for their love of young people and their desire to contribute to their lives. In our research we have encountered only a handful of schools that took the time to gather significant student feedback on their teachers' style, classroom leadership, and general climate issues of the school.

The staff at a certain middle school facilitates a beautiful example of this practice. Twice a year students who wish to are given the opportunity to write a letter of appreciation to any school staff member who may have made a difference in their lives.

We have a tradition here on campus where students are asked to select people that have really made a difference for them and write a letter. It happens a couple times a year. Students are encouraged to sit down and write letters to different people in the school. It may be the secretary, the custodian, teachers, etc. . . . The student can send it to whomever they want, and if a student doesn't want to do it, they don't have to.

I'll receive letters from kids who I don't really know who they are. They'll indicate to me, "You stopped and you said something to me that really meant a lot." For me, it was just an action; for them, it was something they hadn't experienced.

Teachers look forward to these letters. The teachers save the letters; they keep them to read. Often they will receive a letter from someone that will totally surprise them. I seldom hear of anyone who doesn't receive one. Everyone is receiving one.

—Middle School Principal

The beauty of this practice is that it also creates an opportunity to acknowledge everyone contributing to the school, such as the yard duty volunteer, custodians, cafeteria workers, therapists, tutors, bus drivers, and instructional assistants, who often feel invisible in the system and very rarely benefit from any inclusion.

Another principal shared a very creative practice of sending singing telegrams on Valentine's Day. Those telegrams are sung by groups of students in appreciation of teachers' and principals' efforts. The telegrams can be ordered by anyone on the school campus and present a very kind gesture of appreciation:

> *On Valentine's Day, kids are able to send singing telegrams to other people on campus. Student volunteers (singers) are coordinated by a teacher. They'll receive a request to sing and go to that class. We'll have four or five teams of kids singing in different places. We have kids who are sending singing telegrams to their teachers. One day I was stopped in the office by these three girls, who gave me a card from someone and started singing to me a cappella. It was wonderful, beautiful, and uplifting.*

Although appreciation can certainly be spontaneous rather than structured, we believe a more formatted system can generate a climate where people develop the habit of showing acknowledgment. Some other ways for educators to gather positive feedback and appreciation from students and parents are to:

- Conduct a survey on positive aspects of classroom/ school procedures and projects.
- Facilitate class discussions on appreciated aspects of teacher/class relationships, whether facilitated by principal, teacher, or parent.
- Create a playful yet sincere report card for teachers and/or principals.
- Have a response form on notes sent home where parents could ask questions and share gratitude.
- Have a class box where kids could leave notes for the principal to share with teachers at staff meetings or put into their mailboxes.

These broader practices of acknowledgment can offer the advantage of creating a sense of community for everyone.

Appreciation Specifically for Teachers

Often principals and sometimes superintendents make great efforts to appreciate teachers.

One superintendent and his district staff were even able to give gift certificates to a local restaurant to each employee as a token of appreciation. Others prefer to offer small tokens of appreciation informally, as described in the following principals' examples:

We look for ways to celebrate everyone's success. Our school has an Apple Award. It is presented from one teacher to another teacher. Each month it would be passed on, and the teacher passing it tells the staff why before presenting it. Reasons for receiving the award might be for asking for support because someone had a tough week, for sharing information and/or curriculum, among other things. People worked really hard to not let cliques influence the award. It wasn't coming from me, so that there wasn't any competition or evaluation.

I've just started this new practice where at every staff meeting I randomly pick two names, and everyone in the staff has to write a note of appreciation or a comment to those two people. I've noticed that the chosen teachers, so far, have walked out of the meeting really uplifted.

This year I'm really paying attention to the celebration of our successes. I want to start a Thank You Board in the staff room. I am hoping that as people pass by, they might get into the habit of spontaneously writing down something they are grateful for, a thank you to the custodian or to someone they've received help from.

We have a basket that we pass around at staff meetings where people can write an anonymous note and throughout the meeting we randomly share them.

This last practice is particularly meaningful, as it creates a context of appreciation that is truly genuine. No one is obligated to force himself or herself to write something about someone they barely know. The voluntary choice of writing in itself guarantees that what will be written will be very real and received in a powerful way.

Self-Appreciation

In the end, the most important form of acknowledgment is self-appreciation. Self-appreciation develops naturally in environments that are supportive and provide various forms of approval.

When staff set personal goals for themselves that are not academic, they give themselves permission to focus on personal growth as well as the curriculum. This can even be done in small teams of four teachers, for example, where they could assist each other in noticing events that fit each teacher's goal of developing his or her preferred self. This process could be particularly important for experienced teachers who may enjoy new challenges to keep alive their enthusiasm for their profession. Succeeding at one's own established goals certainly promotes self-appreciation and a sense of accomplishment.

Appreciation for
Other Members of the School Community

Secondary staff should also be included in a process of recognition. It can be painful for them to be (unintentionally) excluded from yearbooks, T-shirt distribution, and parties.

The more appreciated and welcome they feel in the school community, the more committed they will be.

Although often invisible, these staff members can contribute in significant ways to children's lives and the school community.

I had a cafeteria manager who had to go in for surgery. I sent her flowers and was glad I did, because I soon noticed how smoothly it runs when she's here!

Appreciation of Principals

Last, but certainly not least, principals should also be the recipients of appreciation and engaged in the experience of appreciation. Principals and authority figures tend to receive less appreciation in general. People can feel intimidated when approaching them, perhaps because of a problem story about the principal not needing feedback or that it would be insulting to comment on a superior's performance.

One principal speaks of her transition from teacher to principal:

That's been the hardest thing. When you leave the classroom where kids will hug and love you and parents are constantly telling you how good a job you are doing, you come into this job and nobody tells you. It's very rare that I get a compliment, so it's very special when it happens.

Boss's Day is one of the rare, structured days when people are reminded of the possibility of expressing appreciation to their principals. Otherwise, principals who have an open-door policy and maintain trusting, honest relationships with the community may receive little droplets of appreciation here and there. Ultimately, principals have to find their own ways of experiencing or detecting appreciation, whether from a child's smile or a staff's trust or a parent's respectful communication style.

When we shared the positive results of our survey with principals, which included reverence for them from their staff, some of them were tearful. Some principals commented on how they do so much and can only guess at how it is appreciated. Our kind words and summaries were very meaningful to them. Although many principals are hesitant to ask for feedback, it can become part of the end-of-the-school-year ritual for principals to pass out a slip and anonymously ask teachers' suggestions or what they most appreciated about the leadership of the school. This builds in a bidirectional communication model based on appreciation.

SELF-REFLECTION

No one does their best thinking on fast forward . . . speed kills great ideas. The faster we speed up, the less time we have to think, to incubate, to ponder, to dream . . . in schools the answer has always been more important than the thought process.

—Reiman, 2000

The current educational system does not allow for reflection time for either teachers or students. As discussed by Peter Senge (O'Neil, 1995), many educators are advocating cooperative learning for students but seeing teaching as individualistic work and are not taking the same stance for themselves. He believes that creating a safe environment in which teachers can reflect on what they are doing, rediscover what they really care about, and learn more about what it takes to work as teams is crucial for teachers to succeed in their profession.

Principals may have only sporadic opportunities to reflect, given that they begin the school year earlier than everyone else and are able to leave the campus occasionally for some "alone time."

Everyone needs time to reflect. Time for reflection is important, as it allows for refueling, connecting with a purpose, reviewing accomplishments, processing mistakes, examining congruency with one's values, and ultimately self-improvement.

The main advantages of self-reflection include:

- Time to explore ways of being that fit who you truly want to be
- Becoming grounded in one's values
- Clarifying goals and intentions
- Learning from mistakes and planning different responses to challenges
- Slowing down to a relaxed place of more peace
- Becoming more able to be attentive and relate to others
- Integrating the lessons of life

Self-reflection can be encouraged in numerous ways and integrated in schools' practices, for teachers and students, without it becoming overly time-consuming.

Self-reflection is a great antidote to many of the negative specifications mentioned in Chapter 1. It allows space for people to decompress from control, dedication, responsibility, and the pressure of being an expert or good role model. The space provides for reenergizing, nurturing, and maintaining a relaxing connection with oneself. All the specifications require that educators be overly outwardly focused. Self-reflection allows for inner concentration. It can be a time to make peace or a time to make plans. Self-reflection can "reboot one's system"; it can reconnect educators with broader visions of themselves: Greater perspective can be obtained, and the challenges of the day can be reevaluated as relatively small in the grand scheme of things.

There are numerous ways to incorporate self-reflection in the school lives of educators. This can be done at transitory moments during a school year, such as the beginning, the end of a quarter or a semester, or at the end of the year.

Teachers should be paid from August to June so that they can talk and review. You can't reflect when you are on the treadmill running through the school year. You can't become a better hitter during the baseball game. It's when you practice and experiment ahead of time that you'll improve.

—Middle School Assistant Principal

Another example might be for educators to make very concrete personal goals at the start of the school year, such as: "I want to attach myself to a student who is struggling or whom I could easily dislike"; "I will reach out to two colleagues I don't know well and connect with them as persons"; or "I will be more patient with students who struggle with reading." These are goals that are very congruent with personal values and promote self-growth as a human and as an educator.

Some schools find ways of including a weekly period of reflection for both their teachers and their students.

The teachers here have been requesting yoga classes for some time. We finally requested it as part of a grant and got it! We all need stress reduction, we have so many things on our plates and try to serve so many people, we really need time to reflect on ourselves. Children also need to learn to reduce stress. They have to know how to help themselves relax and get under control, whether it's on the playground or for class presentations. It's a way of giving them more ownership of their lives, too.

—Elementary School Principal

A variety of means can also be used to incorporate self-reflection in daily lives of teacher. It does not have to be time-consuming, as long as people make a commitment to focus inwardly on their state of being.

We have often offered stress reduction workshops for teachers where they could become engaged in a meditation, a body scan, or a relaxing visualization. This was sometimes scheduled at lunch, but most frequently was facilitated during staff meetings so that no additional demands were placed on staff time. Often we would generate a list of stress-reduction strategies and reconnect teachers with their own coping methods and preferred selves. These occasional workshops were always appreciated and successful.

Self-reflection is also useful for teachers to connect with their own past experiences as students, to remember what it was like to be young and keep that in mind while encouraging current students in academic endeavors.

DEALING WITH THE SYSTEM: TESTING AND UNIONS

The current educational system in the United States is obviously fraught with many problems, many of which, unfortunately, are unlikely to change in the near future. Educators therefore need to learn to function in the best possible ways within that structure, creating space for different experiences. Principals and teachers must find ways to honor and respect their preferences and values while still satisfying the state requirements.

Testing

Certain schools have had the liberty to decide whether they would subject themselves to the pressures of assessment and scores. Although remarkable and certainly advantageous for teachers and students, this is not a luxury that all schools can afford. Educators trapped in a district that values scores might still retain the liberty to choose the extent to which they will let the pressure affect them and their students. Principals can also have an influence on the extent to which these pressures will affect their staff, as described by the following principal:

I see myself as a big filter between the district and my teachers. For example, the district may give us assessment priorities. I will absorb it all, reflect on it, and then present it in a way that's manageable and workable for my staff.

Our colleagues Richard Prinz and Cindy Gowen now work at a school where extensive games and silly activities are organized at breaks and lunch during testing week to help everyone relax. It really changes the climate of that week for students and teachers alike.

At one extreme there are educators who suffer the most and feel that their job depends on the score, while at the other are educators who subject themselves and their students to the score without making a big deal of it, as illustrated in this principal's statement:

If we did a picture that is a puzzle of you and your body, only one small puzzle piece is your standardized test score.

Principals can at least choose not to emphasize the importance of scores. In that way, they avoid the vast majority of the negative effects. This, of course, has to be made public and explained to parents, as well as which other priorities the school decides to embrace.

Unions

Schools are also structured with certain policies and subgroups. Although these may be unavoidable, the ways in which they are exerted can vary greatly. As discussed in the previous chapter, union groups in certain districts are collaborative, useful, and constructive members of school communities. In other districts, however, they are experienced as a waste of finances for teachers (dues) and as heartache for principals. The best that principals can do in these districts is to develop strong connections with the union and have a process of honest collaboration with each other. In addition to that, the staff can decide as a group to hire an external ombudsperson to be available once in a while if conflicts arise between any members of the school community. It is interesting that the service of an ombudsperson is offered in most universities and many companies, yet the only recourse many teachers have in the educational system is often a bureaucratic or antagonistic involvement by the union. The ombudsperson, who does not have a political agenda, offers the advantage of being neutral, objective, simple, cost-effective, and having no other goal than resolving conflicts in the best possible way for both parties.

LEADERSHIP

The only power the principal really has is that of creating a context where everybody, students and adults, can be at their best.

What makes good leaders is not so much what they accomplish, but how they make people feel. In order for administrators to promote such a context, they must be connected to their staff and be in touch with each person's true experience. This idea is in line with newer research on leadership, which has shown that traditional leadership (taking command with a strong voice in front of the group) may not be as effective as once thought. The recent increase in diversity in leaders has rendered visible a variety of approaches to leadership. In particular, networking in more subtle and personalized ways with each individual may in fact be more effective and successful. Such a personalized approach offers the advantage of people feeling heard and seen as a human being *as well as* a worthy and valued member of the community. As stated by Reiman (2000), "Acknowledge people, not their jobs." The success of this leadership style came across very clearly in some schools we visited:

The new principal at our school has done a wonderful job with the staff. She makes sure to touch base with each person in a very genuine way. People can tell she is really interested in them as people and really cares how they are feeling.

The most successful principals in our research were also those who were able to engage their staff in shared meaning and goals. By shared goals, we mean a vision that every member believes in and is committed to contribute to for the good of the community.

Leading teachers to agree on shared goals is certainly a challenging undertaking given the diverse personalities on many staffs and the focus on classroom goals over community. Yet research has shown that people can come together despite their differences to work on a common, meaningful goal or against a common threat. In schools, time must be created for teachers to come together as a community so that each can contribute to a decision regarding a theme for the year, such as diversity, deepening staff relationships and mentoring. A facilitator must be acutely aware of and sensitive to the level of involvement of each individual. For example, when 80% of staff members are interested in a subject but 20% are uninvolved, the outcome could be severely affected.

Aside from these general descriptions of successful leaders, our research showed that in schools, principals were most appreciated when they fulfilled the five criteria below. These five criteria were extracted from our survey's open-ended question regarding principals' actions that contribute to a positive, supportive environment.

Communicate Constructively. Give positive feedback. Encourage frequently, listen, understand, and also acknowledge misunderstandings.

Examples of quotes from surveys include:

- "Gives constructive criticism"
- "Has good communication skills"
- "Shares personal stories"
- "Says positive things (personal and professional)"
- "Gives encouragement, appreciation, and acknowledges efforts"
- "Shares positive growth seen in students"
- "Apologizes when necessary"
- "Maintains good rapport with parents"

Be a Proactive Ally. Provide guidance. Support teachers regarding parent and district office issues, and maintain order at school.

Examples of quotes from surveys include:

- "Supports a teacher when confronted by a parent (right or wrong, the teacher's intentions and efforts should be supported)"
- "Always tries to help if there's a problem in my class"
- "Backs my decisions"
- "Handles serious behavior problems"
- "Comes to parent meetings and supports me in parent discussions"
- "Treats me with respect and stands up for teachers"
- "Presents a strong, visible force on campus, maintaining order and discipline"

Be a Supportive Administrator. Provide needed materials. Encourage professional growth, show interest in teachers and students as humans, be flexible on how to achieve goals, take necessary action to support staff, value teacher and student input, and handle changes cautiously.

Examples of quotes from surveys include:

- "Provides funding for continuing education opportunities"
- "Buys us lunch/treats/water at staff meetings"
- "Covers a class in case of emergency"
- "Supports my teaching style and decisions"
- "Is open minded about change and is flexible on how to achieve goals"
- "Works with us as peers rather than making changes from above and gives us advance warning about upcoming changes"
- "Has a good understanding and promotes schoolwide learning goals"
- "Promotes a team environment"
- "Respects the amount of work you already have and does not add any more to your plate"
- "Often leaves brief notes of appreciation and support after visiting my classroom"

Be Available and Visible. This means the principal is interested in students, interacts with teachers and students, and is there when needed for advice.

Examples of quotes from surveys include:

- "Is always approachable and welcoming"
- "Comes to meetings and parent conferences when invited"
- "Gets kids involved in recess activities"
- "Really knows the children"
- "Takes your class so you can go observe someone else's class"
- "Offers suggestions and support concerning curriculum"

- "Visits my classroom to deliver good news or 'just stopping by'"
- "Answers my questions in a genuine way"
- "Keeps an open door to her office"

Lead With Integrity. Leaders should be persons of their word, returning calls promptly, following through with agreements, being accountable, and taking necessary actions.

Examples of quotes from surveys include:

- "Asks if I need any help or resources and follows through on it"
- "Is a good listener then acts on it"
- "Is really honest with us and can acknowledge mistakes"
- "Has trust in our abilities"
- "Follows through when I ask for assistance"

One of the dangers of power and authority in many professions is a sense of entitlement to disregard others' opinions and a feeling of being above the rules. It is useful for all leaders to ask themselves what method they will use to keep themselves in check. How are they being accountable to others? Are they using power in an appropriate way?

When there is an imbalance of power, there is always a misuse of power, somewhere, somehow (inadvertent or not).

How do you limit the occurrence of misuse of authority?

An example of such effort came from a superintendent we interviewed who told us about a decision that his administration made to be more respectful of principals' time. Although the district office has the power to simply mandate meetings, they have decided to do this different:

One year our assistant superintendent of instruction was trying to visit a particular classroom and found she was too busy. We decided that if she was the lead of instruction and was too busy, that must shed some light on how busy principals are. The next year we canceled principal meetings at the district office, and we visited each principal once a month on their school site for a structured conversation. These conversations included whatever they needed to talk about. "Rather than you meet with us, we'll meet with you." We tried to model a different kind of access and communication. It sent an amazing message about the values here.

With these ingredients, a school culture can resonate with substance and vitality.

In the end, it is not our techniques, our talents, or our knowledge that matter, it is our being.

—W. Bennis (in Bolman & Deal, 2001)

All of these ingredients of a supportive school culture are summarized in Resource C. Although these practices can go very far in eliminating several problems, some of the experiences of pressure and having too much responsibility can remain. For this reason, we will now briefly share specific strategies and words of wisdom from principals who are happily surviving the system!

CHAPTER SEVEN

Practices That Support a Caring School Culture

I n this chapter we will summarize words of wisdom shared by several experienced principals who had developed the following survival strategies in the face of contextual pressures:

1. *Connect, connect, connect.* Do not let the pressures of power, efficiency, and availability push you into isolation. With all the pressures to answer demands from district, parents, and teachers, it is easy to isolate oneself with work. Many principals have attempted that lifestyle in their first year and barely survived. In the end, those who maintained some enthusiasm for their profession were those who networked in meaningful ways with their teachers and connected with students. Ultimately, knowing the names of students and their hobbies, having personal conversations with staff, and using some of the precious and scarce time to network was not only enriching for principals but yielded a greater unity and collaboration in the whole school. This networking was also critical *among* principals, where those who consulted actively with their vice-principal, another principal, a mentor, or a buddy regarding in-school problems felt much more confident, made better decisions, and were less isolated.

I have a core group of principals to go to and I am lucky to have my vice-principal, otherwise I'd be in total isolation.

—Middle School Principal

You can't be afraid to go to bocce ball with your staff or go in the staff room and talk and joke with them. You've got to be seen as a human, as a person. Then they find out . . . He doesn't have all the answers. He's not God sitting up there in his office!

—Middle School Principal

2. *Name the pressure.* Talk about your experience to trusted colleagues. Pressures are most oppressive when they are invisible and unquestioned. The easiest way to tackle them is, once again, to externalize the problematic pressure and map its effects, as explained in Chapter 2 of this book. Once aware of and clear about the situation, you can make a choice as to other ways of being and can explore your comfort zone.

In some cases you can even invite the whole staff to explore the effects of a certain pressure and list strategies used by everyone to minimize its harmful effects. We have visited schools where everyone secretly resented what was assumed to be a group expectation. Yet when asked in confidence or surveyed anonymously, most of the staff were against that expectation! When made visible, certain pressures can be redefined and/or softened greatly.

3. *Consciously limit the impact of pressures by remembering that you do have multiple identities.* You are a principal, a person, a friend, maybe an intimate partner and a parent.

I live 45 minutes away [from school] and that is by choice. It does feel more comfortable to me knowing I can not shave a day or put on my gardening shorts and go to the store without worrying about parents and kids seeing me.

—Middle School Principal

Make a choice as to when you can let go of pressures and when you have to fulfill them. Be clear with yourself and even with employees that, as a principal, it is your responsibility to take specific actions, even if, as a person, you really dislike an action (e.g., asking a teacher to leave). Some of our principals would even specify as they spoke that they were putting on a principal hat or that they were taking it off. When a principal makes it visible that he or she is taking off the principal hat (e.g., the hat of evaluation), the principal becomes more accessible, real, and human. Principals may intend to "take off the hat," but if they do not articulate it verbally, people may not notice the change because of the differential of power. If you let people know "I'm going to take off this hat," it creates a different kind of communication.

4. *Resist the temptation associated with the pressure of power to have "your fingers" on everything.* If the district makes controversial decisions or the staff is divided by educational differences, engage a mediator or facilitate the discussion in a neutral way so that each perspective can feel heard. Ultimately, if you favor an educational practice but no one else does, you have to be ready to be patient or to let it go. The staff has to be willing to engage in a practice on their own for the practice to be successful.

> *You can't change overnight. I work with those teachers who want to [change] and you build a successful program slowly. I look for ways to support people that are taking little tiny steps. I work with the people who are in favor of [an innovative new idea] and let their success speak for itself. I would say, "Go ahead. You really believe in this, go ahead!"*
>
> —Elementary School Principal

This principal told us how she was intrigued with the idea of teachers looping with their classes. This means a teacher keeps the same class of students two years in a row and teaches each year's curriculum. The staff read articles about the process and did other research to determine if it would be beneficial to them. One teacher chose to loop from kindergarten to first grade, and she could not stop talking about how wonderful it was. The principal reported that, all of the sudden, there were many people willing to try it.

Another principal speaks of the difficulty of letting go of situations and issues on campus. This could be anything from what is happening in the cafeteria to seeing a child with whom he had really connected in trouble with the assistant principal:

> We want to have our finger on the pulse of what's going on at school. You have to delegate and let go of some of that control to other people. It's hard for us to do as principals because we're supposed to have that power and control over things. You have to keep your good faith in other people and even if they [make mistakes] along the way, it's part of learning.

—Middle School Principal

5. *Simply accept that you will never fulfill the pressure of doing it all.* Find your own personal standards for what counts as "having accomplished something" at the end of your day. It is most likely that, of all the items you planned to accomplish at the beginning of the day, many will remain incomplete. Know, however, that unfinished paperwork will remain just that, while an unattended relationship will swell with resentment.

> I have to be proud of what I did accomplish. Whatever paper you miss will always come back to you. However, if you leave [the district/education] tomorrow, you still need to have your relationships, your friends, your spouse, and your kids. Fifty years down the road when you end your career or [are] on your deathbed that's who will be with you. I try never to lose sight of that.

—Elementary School Principal

> I often set myself three little goals for the day and make sure I accomplish them before I leave, which I've decided is 5 P.M. I make the choice to spend time with my wife every day

and sacrifice a half a day on the weekend to have a quiet paperwork period.

—Middle School Principal

You can always say, "Gee, I'll get back to you. Thank you for your opinion." Unless it's blood and guts you don't have to solve it immediately. The thing you learn as a new principal is that the only thing you really have to get to right away is blood and guts. Then you call 911. (laughs)

—Elementary School Principal

6. *Realize that the pressures tend to make you ultimately responsible for everything, while in reality you can delegate.* So many responsibilities can be trusted to the hands of others. Staff or parents, when appropriate, may appreciate the opportunity to be in charge of a specific assignment or to be an administrator for an hour while the principal attends to other necessities.

I've realized that I can delegate many items. For example, I asked the librarian to be in charge of the surveys reviewing our services. It's her department, she's excited to do it, and it frees my time for other issues.

—Elementary School Principal

7. *Remember to keep some perspective on the pressure of power and the misleading stories it promotes.* Redefine the power differential as a difference of roles.

Really we are all on the same team but just have different roles.

—Middle School Principal

The kids here have a realistic view of me. They get to know me inside and outside of the classroom and on the playground. They call me by my first name, which helps.

—Elementary School Principal

Power is how you react.

—Elementary School Principal

8. *Although the pressure of efficiency pushes you to accomplish more and more as quickly as possible, give yourself permission to think and be in touch with the school community and your role as a leader.*

If you really want to be collaborative in your decisions, then it does take longer, and in general there really are decisions you can postpone. Other times, if I have to make a decision, I'll leave campus to get a sandwich and it gives me time to think.

—Elementary School Principal

You could sit, listen to voice mail, and answer e-mail all day. You could sit and react to things all day. Or you could decide you are going to get out there for two hours a day and be a leader. Hopefully it's your collective vision and you will stay with that vision.

—Elementary School Principal

9. *Use your sense of humor to keep some perspective on those unrealistic pressures.* There are times where it is important to laugh at the impossibility of doing it all.

We have a serious job to do, but humor is a big part of my life and if I can't laugh at myself, I'll be in trouble.

—Elementary School Principal

10. *Finally, hold on to your values and preferred visions of yourself.* Why were you attracted to the field of education in the first place? What were your hopes and dreams? What is energizing for you in your role? The following are additional educators' survival tricks in the face of pressures:

Keep breathing and stay present.

Take a quiet walk every morning before coming to school.

Notice positive encounters with students.

Ask questions of your colleagues to see where they are really *at.*

Remember, everyone has a story of feeling out of place. You are not alone.

CHAPTER EIGHT

Working With Parents and Volunteers

I n this final chapter we will generalize the ideas presented throughout this book to address issues with other adults working in schools. We will first discuss the presence of parents and their relationships, at times problematic, with teachers. We will then end with the transcript of a workshop facilitated with yard duty volunteers at the request of a concerned principal.

PROBLEM STORIES OF PARENTS AND BATS

News Flash: Seemingly overnight the Austin City Council was faced with a dilemma . . . their new and architecturally innovative bridge was invaded by bats. The humans considered possibilities. They could keep them out, control their comings and goings or . . . welcome their presence. The people soon discovered that welcoming bats into their environment could be quite an asset, despite initial fears and mythical stories. In the end, the presence of bats enriched the community in terms of education, activities, and financial gains.

Some of you may not appreciate bats because of the numerous negative stories you may have been exposed to as a youngster. As an adult, you may reluctantly concede the fact that bats are actually an important part of many habitats, reduce certain problems in many ecosystems, and deserve respect.

This is only one of many examples of a community welcoming another group of beings and being enriched by their presence. Could the same parallel be drawn with the historical exclusion of parents?

There has been a growing trend for schools to involve parents instead of exclude them.

It used to be that the principal's job was to keep the parents out; now you need to bring them in, embrace them, and not try to avoid it. It's the only salvation for the public school system.

—School District Superintendent

Parents are typically excluded from the classroom because of a problem story based on a series of fears and misconceptions (see Figure 8.1). This problem story may get teachers to

- Fear that parents will not be responsive, reliable, responsible, and suited for work with children
- Be concerned about parents' evaluations, misperceptions, and gossip about their work
- Fear that extra time will be needed to manage these additional people in the classroom, the context where teachers are already overwhelmed by limited time and large numbers of students waiting for directions

These fears become intricately organized into a problem story, which exaggerates the likelihood and frequency of problem events and makes invisible any alternative stories about parents, which may include rich experiences of collaboration and helpfulness. These stories have the general effect of reducing collaboration between many teachers and parents in schools.

Figure 8.1   Teachers have a problem story of parents. They mostly see potential problems and are suspicious of the good intentions

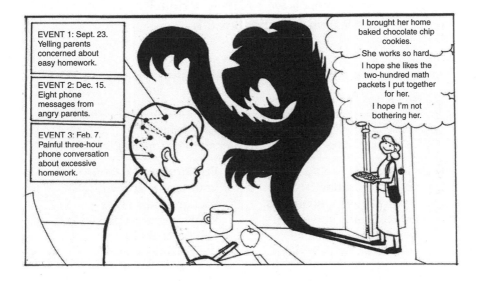

For years, I really struggled with parent help. I had some parents who wanted to work in my class, but I didn't know them well and kept hearing from other teachers how parents frequently gossip and how they flake out when you are counting on them. A colleague next door to me always had parents in her room and she was always running around like a maniac, trying to keep them busy. I kept a little stack of papers in the back of the room for parents to correct in the library or some masters to copy at the office. This way I was addressing their need to work in the class, but I didn't really have to have them underfoot. I felt awful about it. It really wasn't how I wanted it, but honestly, they made me nervous.

—Third Grade Teacher

The existence of a problem story about parents is made evident by comparing results from our surveys. In our research, teachers' problem stories of parents in traditional versus parent-participation schools led to strikingly different comments.

Teachers from parent-participation schools usually expressed appreciative comments that were varied and rich about building a collaborative relationship with parents, whereas remarks from more traditional schools were narrow, scripted, and dealt mostly with communication skills. See Box 8.1.

Box 8.1

Advice From a More Traditional School	*Advice From a Parent-Participation School*
• Use good communication (newsletters, phone calls, notes home, and e-mail as much as possible) • Get to know their name RIGHT away and use it • Have a firm handshake and look them in the eye when meeting • Start with the positive first • Be proactive • Be careful what you say; it will be repeated • They can be your best partner or your worst rival • Remember you are in charge; know where to draw the line • Get parents involved as volunteers but don't expect miracles • Respond in a professional manner • You can't win them all!	• Feel free to talk about your family and your background so they know you are a person • Tell them about yourself—open up • One of the most important jobs is to be sure parents have input. A teacher needs to hear what parents have to say and be open-minded • Let them know they are valuable and important! Let them know that their participation in their child's education is important! • Respect their experience as parents • Be inviting and inclusive • Don't lose your backbone and pretend you know what you are doing even if you don't • Try to remain open and positive even when parents are not; find common ground and listen

Parents may also have their own problem stories. Parents, especially those who are minorities or from underprivileged backgrounds, may have a story about teachers being unapproachable. Parents fundamentally want the best for their child and may be ambivalent about stepping in because of fear of retaliation or judgment. Parents may also possess a problem story about feeling unwelcome in schools. These stories contribute to a lower volunteer rate than what would truly serve schools.

The following are two examples; the first from an elementary school principal and the second from a parent:

I remember when I was a volunteer in my child's class. Recess came and I had to go sit outside on the bench, then I'd go back in the classroom when the bell rang. I was not invited into the staff room. Teachers had coffee and relaxed in the staff room and talked with their friends in the staff room, which was totally off limits to us. I think that is one of the bad things that continue in this day and age. Teachers think that they deserve to have a break from parents, but with that mentality, how can you ever work in partnership to educate? Particularly if you have people there that are giving up their time.

I was told at school that they didn't allow parents in the class room and that they only wanted help from parents with fundraising. This felt like a major discount of what I could bring into the equation and asked for a set of skills I neither have nor care to develop. Also, I wondered what were they hiding that they didn't allow parents in the classrooms?

PARENT INVOLVEMENT: FROM PROBLEM STORY TO COLLABORATION

The most obvious and beneficial way to increase a sense of community and reduce problem stories is to involve parents.

Schools have a variety of policies regarding parental involvement. Some schools require a minimum number of hours of parent involvement, others welcome parent volunteers as helpers, some schools prefer that parents do not remain in the classroom, and still others are begging for help.

As discussed earlier, there are problem stories that exist around relationships with parents. For most public schools, the first step to increasing parent involvement is to process with teachers their beliefs about parent involvement and to support a gradual exploration of parent involvement.

> *When I have a teacher who is not so comfortable with parents being in the classroom, I have the teacher wean them in, an hour a week or so. I have them work in the copy room helping the teacher copy papers, then slowly as the teacher becomes more comfortable with the parent, I suggest the parent come in and run a reading group or something in the class.*
>
> —Elementary School Principal

> *Involving parents is a "ground-up" change in a school. Teachers need to understand that this is not something that is happening to them; they are a part of the change. Without their active involvement and support, it will not be successful. Teachers become so autonomous, so you have to lead them by giving lots of examples of successful programs, reading books about parent participation, and having discussions about why it works. You also need a parent group ready to go.*
>
> —Parent Participation Elementary School Principal

> *Teachers need to understand that when parents want to be involved that does not mean that we want to take over their job or critique their teaching. Well, most of us anyway. We want to support them as teachers; we want to show our kids that school is important, enough for us to spend time there. We want to provide extra adult assistance for the students.*
>
> —Parent of an Elementary School Student

Many individuals who have had the opportunity to deconstruct and examine these fears have come to the following conclusion: "For every one parent who causes trouble, there are 29 others who help in many ways."

The second step is to establish a helpful parental infrastructure not only to welcome parents, especially if they are from an underprivileged minority group, but also to coordinate their activities in a way that is helpful to the school and meaningful to the parent.

Work and issues of embarrassment keep parents from schools. Parents may not have been comfortable in schools as children and still feel that. It's good to make them comfortable and slowly build the relationship. People will come on campus if their kids bring them. So we try to bring people together for important things, like family reading night. This gets them to be more comfortable here. We'll go from there.

—Elementary School Principal

We worked with two BAFTTA (Bay Area Family Therapy Training Associates) interns who hosted parties for their students' families at a community day school. Many of these families felt disconnected from school, so they were all invited together to socialize and have fun. It was made very clear that there would be no problem talk and no mention of any recent trouble with any student. The student's "ticket" to get into the party and the "movie room" was to bring his or her parent(s). It was an overwhelming success, with requests from all the families to do it again.

Parent involvement in schools is determined by the parents' interests and requires a lot of work on the part of the administration and educators.

It takes a lot of work and a conscious effort to match parents with their strengths, to match their schedules, and to give them really meaningful tasks in the classroom. Teachers must be willing to be flexible and adjust to parents being in the classroom, knowing in the long run it will make their program that much more meaningful. A lot of teachers are not comfortable with being observed and it does change the dynamics when visitors come; yet a teacher does have to be comfortable teaching in a fishbowl. In my opinion, it's a professional duty because you should be teaching that way anyway.

—Elementary School Principal

What I am trying to do is set a culture that welcomes parents and supports them. Those really involved parents are invited in. We are now coordinating them. I want them to be doing more than stapling papers and running dittos. Schools need to open up activities that are meaningful to parents, such as working with kids, teaching, helping with reading intervention, and assisting with school plays. They can be working with kids, and we should train them on how to do that, including what is confidential.

—Middle School Principal

There is growing evidence that school communities greatly benefit from parent involvement. There are advantages for all groups of people involved: teachers, students, and parents.

Advantages for Teachers

When educators are able to shrink the problem, they are able to see parents as teammates in the education of children, and a variety of interactions become possible. Teachers are less isolated and gain valuable support on multiple levels.

On a relational level, teachers and parents can have adult conversations, share enjoyable moments, support each other in difficult situations, and witness the complexity and beauty of classroom interactions.

On a functional level, teachers can delegate some of the work, assign subgroups of children to another adult, teach a more child-centered curriculum, have more possibilities of addressing specific needs, share the organizing and supervising of celebrations and field trips, be more able to launch exciting and special projects, and benefit from a variety of adults' special talents and expertise, such as computer expertise.

One parent shared the extensive jobs she had taken on at her children's school:

I have worked with small groups of children, mostly on math, but also on reading, discussion and language. I have lead groups on science investigation and have created and run cooking workshops with the help of two other parents. I have driven and chaperoned on field trips. I have also helped with special art projects and been a literacy tutor for struggling readers, under the guidance of a curriculum specialist who trained me.

An added benefit is that parent volunteers see what is going on in the class and become stronger advocates for the school.

Advantages for Students

Children benefit greatly from the presence of their own and other parents in the classroom. They feel supported in their academic challenges, safer in the face of peer conflicts, and engaged in creative projects. In addition, children have reported appreciating simply having the presence of their parents in schools. Parent participation can increase students' exposure to adults from minority groups and convey a context where students learn to value diversity.

It's no secret that kids that have involved parents do well at school.

—School District Superintendent

Advantages for Parents

Parents who are involved in their child's classroom become more connected to their child, as their relationship is enriched by the shared experience of an important journey. They can gain a better understanding of their child's experience of school, peer and teacher interactions, and the curriculum.

When parents are involved, they not only develop a realistic perspective of the challenges of education but also can take action on problems they witness. When schools exclude parents, one of the ways parents might express their dissatisfaction can be to criticize teachers and principals. If you invest time and energy in an institution, you feel a sense of belonging to it, and it becomes uncomfortable to slander that to which you belong. Parents whose children may struggle with a trouble habit may also gain important insights into their child's challenges instead of oscillating between wanting to protect their child and trusting the adult in charge. This can be particularly true for minority families, who may wonder whether their child's constant discipline is a result of racism or the consequence of actual misbehaviors.

Parents who may have less confidence in their parenting abilities because of social status or other life experiences can experience a school's welcoming of their contributions as uplifting, validating their parenting abilities and strengthening their preferred stories of being caring, worthy, and knowledgeable parents.

> *We had a couple of meetings where we brought in parents for schoolwide meetings. We explained this whole life skills program which tied in with this social awareness curriculum. We explained the class rules and showed these words (responsibility, motivation, respect, etc.) and we said to them, "What do these words mean to you?" They met together and talked and shared what the words meant to their family. It was an amazing conversation. It was amazing because most of the parents had never been asked to participate in a dialogue with teachers like this. They were excited to be having a conversation but also it made them realize they had a lot to offer their kids. A lot of these parents would tend to discount what they have to offer compared with what the school has to offer. It also was to show that we have similar values. There are certain universal ones we can agree on.*

—Fifth Grade Teacher

WHEN CONFLICTS ARISE

When an educator is in an authentic relationship with parents, conflicts may be solved more easily. The following ideas have been helpful to the participants in our research when interacting with parents:

1. See parents as knowledgeable allies.

   Parents are their child's best advocates 99% of the time. Listen to what they know and understand, what they see as the complexity of the situation, and what kind of educational environment their child should be in. If you understand all of these things and try to be proactive, not reactive, if you value their input, and work with them, they are your best allies.

   —School District Superintendent

2. Be open to cultural differences.

   It is really an ongoing exercise to see if teachers can overcome their biases. I once had a teacher who came to my office quite upset because she had a conference with a father who promised he would read with his son each day, but found out the family was not reading together. She didn't understand why he wouldn't do it. Later my friend visited, who worked with this particular father. She said he was in tears each morning because he couldn't read with his child. I went back to the teacher to discuss this matter. The teacher said, "He told me he could do it!" I responded, "Do you think he wants to sit with an educator and admit that he can't read with his son? To admit that he may be literate in his own country but not here? Of course not! Do you know how embarrassing that is?"

   —Elementary School Principal

3. Be realistic and take notes. Document meetings with parents for future reference.

   I keep a detailed account of dialogues or problem-focused conversations that have occurred with parents. It gives me some protection when conflicts arise and also refreshes my memory of previous agreements.

   —Elementary School Principal

4. Accept the unpredictability of parents, and be aware of your needs *and* theirs.

Interaction with parents is a very complex part of teaching. I have to meet a large number of parents' needs and talk to them from where they are. That's a complex and difficult thing. I know what I'm doing in the classroom. I never really know what I'm doing with an adult. Every inter-action is like, "What's going on next? How am I going to react to that? What are my emotions? What are their emo-tions?" With adults, you never know what you are going to see. There's just an endless variety of person. That makes it quite an interesting job.

—First Grade Teacher

5. Put yourself in their shoes and remember that they passionately want the best for their child(ren).

I know these parents are young and anxious. The parents here are particularly overanxious and striving. I remember when my kids were little, I was anxious, so I really under-stand that sentiment where you want the best for your child and that this teacher will be the one to prevent your child from going to Stanford. Once I had kids of my own, it was more humbling. I realized what these parents are going through. That doesn't mean the way I approach it is any different, but I am more understanding of where they are coming from.

—Second Grade Teacher

I had an opportunity to work in high S.E.S. [socioeconomic-status] schools and poverty-stricken schools. What I got out of that is, that parents, no matter what their S.E.S. level is, no matter what their level of education or the parent language, all parents want their children to have something better than what they had when they were kids.

—Elementary School Principal

*I always try to remember to relate to parents as parents,
and remember they are talking as a mother or a father who
is intensely preoccupied with their child's well-being.*

—Elementary School Principal

6. Remember the humanity of people and hold on to
   kindness.

*I don't have any trouble, normally, with parents. I don't
have any trouble with any parent, because I do exactly what
I do with the children. I love them, you know, in another
way. I'm kind to them. I encourage them. I care about them.
I listen. It's the same to me. They are just big kids.*

—First Grade Teacher

7. Schedule a home visit, especially if the family is
   culturally different from you. Home visits, although
   time-consuming, have been found to be useful in fostering connection and understanding and in preventing
   problems.

*If you meet someone in [their] own home you have a differ-
ent sense of who they are. To have that trusting relationship
is worth it to all these teachers. They get paid for making
these home visits, but they said even if they didn't get paid,
based on what they know now, they would do those home
visits as much as possible. It cements the support they get
from families better than anything else they have ever done.
We had a child who was having severe troubles; he was soil-
ing himself, he always had a runny nose, and he had struggles in class. We were really concerned. The teacher made
a home visit and found out the kid was living in a cardboard shack. So his inability to focus and his sickness were
understood in a different light. The teacher's understanding
of who that child was when he was struggling was different
than this child is lazy and unclean.*

—Elementary School Principal

There are things I say to children that I feel very foolish about afterward, once I see their home and the things they have and don't have. I relate to them differently when I know what their bedroom looks like.

—First Grade Teacher

MORE IDEAS FOR YOUR SCHOOL COMMUNITY

- Unravel the problem stories about parents in an honest staff dialogue
- Articulate advantages and disadvantages of parent presence
- Accept that parents will be present in some way or another, so find a context for them to be there constructively
- Have a parent-volunteer coordinator
- Create arrangements to receive feedback from families and be genuinely interested in listening to families about school experiences
- Have a person from within the community's subculture act as a parent liaison and assist in communication when families speak a different language than the educator's
- Offer workshops for parents (regarding language, parenting, educational issues, etc.)
- Give meaningful tasks to parents
- Make parents feel good about themselves
- Have social events so that families feel connected to the school

WORLD WIDE WEB RESOURCES

http://www.rci.rutgers.edu/~cfis/

The Center for Family Involvement in Schools provides professional development programs and resources that strengthen family-school-community partnerships. The Center is a part of the Rutgers Center for Mathematics, Science, and Computer Education (CMSCE). The Web site provides links to other parental involvement sites and includes information about afterschool programs, family math and science involvement, and professional development workshops.

http://www.gse.harvard.edu/

Harvard Family Research Project (HFRP) promotes child development, student achievement, healthy family functioning, and community development by researching and publishing findings on such topics such as early childhood care, family involvement in education, and community partnerships. The Web site includes information about The Family Involvement Network of Educators (FINE), which is a national network of more than 2,000 people who are interested in promoting strong partnerships between educators and community members.

http://www.ncpie.org/

NCPIE is a coalition of major education, community, public service, and advocacy organizations working to create meaningful family-school partnerships in every school in the United States. The Web site includes a database with hundreds of resources for educators and families.

http://www.csos.jhu.edu/

The National Network of Partnership Schools, established by researchers at Johns Hopkins University, brings together schools, districts, and states that are committed to developing and maintaining comprehensive programs of school-family-community partnerships. The Web site includes partnership program components, a 12-month guide for the work of action groups, and Frequently Asked Questions (FAQ) about school-family-community connections.

YARD DUTY VOLUNTEERS

Yard duty volunteers are another group of people for which we are often consulted. Principals' and teachers' concerns are usually about the appropriateness or helpfulness of yard duty volunteers' interventions. Teachers do not have the time to deal with a student who comes back from recess over and over again angered by an interaction with a yard duty volunteer. Yard duty volunteers in those situations may have good justifications for their actions or helpful intentions, but the result can impede the system instead of helping. For this reason we have on several occasions been invited to speak with those generous volunteers. The two one-hour meetings usually simply have the tone of exploring and sharing their experiences with each other while we ask questions that promote reflection. The following is a summary of the process (which is generally distributed to them after the two meetings).

What Are the Goals of a Yard Duty Volunteer?

- Safety
- Refereeing—teaching kids other ways of resolving conflicts
- Contributing to a context where kids can be happy
- Helping kids solve problems on their own
- Helping kids to stop and think
- Empowering kids to work it out
- Teaching respect

What Does Respect Mean
When You Are in This Role?

- Be physically at their level
- Listen to their stories
- Explain why x, y, or z has to be done
- Be willing to apologize
- Have same expectations of ourselves as we have for them in terms of talking (yelling, tone of voice, words chosen, etc.)

What Are the Values and the Preferred
Ways of Being You Bring to This Job?

- Letting young people know you care
- Remembering that young people are thoughtful, loving, good inside, learning, and that they are CHILDREN!

- Realizing they may not have developed tools
- Realizing there may be problems in their lives
- Realizing there is probably a reason why they do x, y, or z
- Recognizing that ESL students sometimes may feel lonely and lost
- Creating a space for young people to think
- Validating their stories, listening to them
- Letting them know you'll come back to them in a few minutes
- Having them sit
- Being curious
- Using metaphors/examples
- Keeping a sense of humor
- Going for walks

When Do Yard Duty Volunteers Inadvertently Contribute to Problems?

Adults get pulled into doing unhelpful things when frustration gets them into

- Making quick decisions
- Shutting off, not wanting to hear something
- Taking things away over and over again
- Forcing young people to apologize (it's disrespectful and doesn't mean anything)
- Yelling at young people—telling them to "shut up"
- Being impatient
- Repeating rules over and over (there could be something preventing a child from understanding or following the rule)
- Giving advice (which we know generally doesn't work) and being upset when the child doesn't follow it
- Overfocusing on an upsetting event
- Taking a "This is the way it is" attitude

Have You Noticed the Effects of Adults' Frustration on Kids?

- Young people tune out
- They feel misunderstood
- They disconnect
- They give up talking to you
- They walk away
- They don't listen to you anymore
- They become sad, discouraged
- They feel bad about themselves
- They go into a shell
- They lose confidence in themselves
- They get more frustrated, shake their heads, and raise their voices

Adults' frustration/disrespect can escalate the problem and feed a vicious cycle:

Figure 8.2   The vicious cycle of disrespect between adults and students

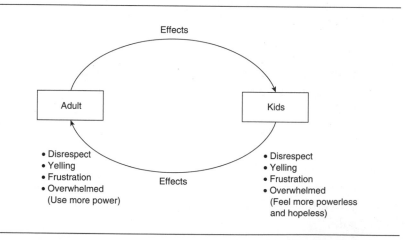

STRATEGIES FOR CHALLENGING SITUATIONS

- Readjust your expectations instead of blowing the whistle day after day

- Have a *conversation* before a conflict arises or when there is less frustration
- Give them a choice: "What would be more helpful now—to sit for a few minutes? Or to talk about it?"
- When appropriate, remove the threat of punishment—it will allow for a more constructive and honest conversation
- Allow each child to explain his or her story while the other listens—and let them know you won't take sides or punish, you just want them to understand each other
- Give them a chance—it will give them some power and the feeling that you care

How Can Adults Hold Onto Their Values / Preferred Ways in Challenging Situations?

- Remember that the more a child struggles with problems, the more he or she needs a recess to play, run, have fun, and let it out. It is the most important time of the day for many unhappy young people. Don't take it away unnecessarily.

- Remember that young people who struggle with problems have many, many adults on their backs, yelling at them and punishing them.

- Remember the teacher who made such a difference in your own life by being kind to you, despite your struggles as a child (e.g., would your favorite teacher ask a lot of questions, listen, raise her voice, ask you what you wanted, be loving, giving, patient? Did this teacher take the time to count to ten under her breath?).

- Have confidence in young people's abilities. Acknowledge them and allow the time necessary.

- Remembering helpful people can perhaps help each one of us to stop the cycle of frustration and to remove ourselves mentally from the situation, reflect/think, and then go back to dealing with it in a fair, caring way.

- Parents, teachers, yard duty volunteers, and children often do the best they can, given the circumstances of their lives.

Conclusion

Questions and Answers

I've tried everything to build a greater cohesiveness with this staff. I've tried conversations, organizing parties, special events, . . . nothing has worked. What more can I do?

Some situations have become so ugly that they seem unsolvable. If some school members become entrenched in destructive patterns of relating and have defeated a variety of problem-resolution efforts, the only option may be to move them. This can happen, however, only after other more constructive attempts, extensive documentation on the issue, and with serious backup from the superintendent. Staff can also be surveyed as to their general ideas on how to solve the current disagreements in their school. Although anonymous, this survey could provide the administration with alternative ideas or at least a sense of support from the rest of the staff. Conversations with the staff then need to take place to explore the effects of this decision and to address any distrust that may grow out of the incident.

Will having a school mission statement help us come together as a group of educators or will it be just another exercise that will be forgotten in the busyness of the year? I have a stable staff of teachers who come back each year. Do we really need to review it?

When everybody contributes to a mission statement and a vision in a meaningful way, they are more likely to be committed to it. Schools whose teachers are vested in very different methods can be invited to discuss when a particular method is useful and when it is not. What are students' reactions to it? Who benefits and who is marginalized? In the end, articulating these ideas will allow for more flexibility and overlap in teachers' approach.

Ultimately a school staff can also be invited into a discussion about diversity and how they determine which differences are contributing to diversity on the staff and which are differences in philosophical ideology that make collaboration too difficult.

I am a principal with teachers on staff who have radically different philosophies. I can't start fresh with a whole new staff of teachers who agree on their philosophy. How do I deal with the vast differences?

A school community needs to learn to process and embrace differences, as opposed to seeking to eliminate them to become a homogeneous culture. Teachers will be exposed to heterogeneity in their students; how can they possibly be respectful of the differences between their students if they struggle with dealing with the differences in their staff?

I am uncomfortable with the decisions made by the district and do not feel that I can speak up much more without endangering my job. I feel very stuck and unhappy.

Ultimately, if a district's philosophy becomes too distant from your own on many levels and for an extended period of time, you have to face a serious decision: stay or leave? Being honest with yourself and exploring the effects of this problem on your life (thoughts, feelings, behaviors; who you are becoming; relationships with staff, friends, or family; your dreams, goals, values) must be done in-depth. When a context is systematically bringing out the worst in you, it may be easier and more gratifying to move on than to continue fighting a losing battle that will destroy you. It is important to talk to someone about these thoughts and perhaps give yourself a deadline for reevaluation of the improvements achieved, if any. You might remember an intimate relationship where you were miserable for a long time, then left, discovered life again, and ended up wondering why you did not leave earlier. Sometimes the miserable but familiar seems more comfortable than the novel unknown, especially as we grow older. Yet the self you once were that was willing to take risks and explore the world is still in you, somewhere; buried perhaps, but still retrievable if you reconnect with its memory.

There is a teacher in our school who seems a bit burned out by the profession. She used to participate in meetings, mentor younger teachers, and really care about her students. Now she seems grumpy and negative. Last year I gave her a bad evaluation, hoping to motivate her, but it just made her more resentful. What should I do?

Devoted teachers can burn out very quickly in public schools nowadays. Those who survive long years have either developed intricate ways of reenergizing themselves or have become burned out, disconnected, and tired. Principals, who are often at a loss as to how to motivate some of these teachers, may resort to the only power they seem to have: evaluation. Unfortunately this usually alienates the teachers and causes further resentment. Even if these teachers would like to change and have the best of intentions, they will feel misunderstood, unfairly judged, and further discouraged in their work. In this situation, the best possible scenario is one where a compassionate conversation can be held with the teacher, gently making visible her decreased enthusiasm for her work. If the conversation is supportive and collaborative, the teacher may be able to articulate what blocks or constraints actually stifle her performance. Once those blocks are named, a plan of action can be created that, hopefully, will remove or at least reduce those blocks. Ultimately most people, younger and older, need support rather than punishment when they engage in troublesome behavior.

I have a teacher who is harassing students, yet no parents have complained. My hands are tied because I can't document the problem. How is it that students and parents are not complaining about this offensive issue?

Parents and students are often fearful of retaliation if they speak of a problem that involves hierarchy. A teacher can be seen as the powerful one in a classroom, with no other adults as witnesses or protectors. Parents and young people may be worried that the teacher's mistreatment may simply worsen if they speak up and that students will suffer from an even greater experience of disrespect and unfairness.

It is always important to talk with the teacher who is scrutinized and explore his or her intentions or understanding of the situation. Sometimes the problem story results from a misunderstanding or a mistake. If this is the case, it can hopefully be resolved through conversation. If the problem is actually occurring and is harmful, this will at least inform the teacher that the problem is now named and will be under investigation. Sometimes that is all that is needed to reduce the frequency of the harmful behavior.

In a school where the context is one of respect, students will feel more empowered to make their voices heard and will express their concerns to trusted adults. Teachers who are in this situation will already be thinking and practicing in non-hierarchical ways and be inspired to make changes in their philosophy of interacting with young people. When parents are involved in a school, they also witness classroom interactions and may be in a better position to demand accountability, or at least to feel less intimidated about speaking up. Principals who cannot rely on these resources must resort to evaluation and documentation of the concerns and hopefully involve their superintendent in exploring remediation or transfer possibilities.

What happened to Karen, John, and Chris, who struggled with issues in the very first chapter?

Perhaps you would like to try to solve these dilemmas yourself. How would you apply the ideas in this book to those problematic situations?

Here are our solutions: You might remember that Karen yelled at her students and struggled with feeling like a fraud. A discussion was facilitated with the whole staff around such questions as: "How many of you have done something against your better judgment as a teacher?" "How many of you end up yelling even though you would really rather not?" In this process it became visible for Karen, as well as for many others, that they all struggled with Impatience at times and that Impatience could make them act against their preferred values. Impatience was then externalized, and its effects were mapped on thoughts, feelings, behaviors, relationships with students, experiences, and identities. Contexts that were more likely to invite Impatience were discussed, and strategies everyone had developed to remain connected with their preferred selves were shared. The staff ended the meeting with a determination to observe their own successes and strategies for avoiding Impatience for the following two weeks. When they gathered again, almost everyone shared new ways they had used to remain connected with their values. Several of the staff also acknowledged that sometimes Impatience had crept in despite their best intentions. In the end everyone agreed that they would keep trying but that it was impossible to completely eradicate Impatience in certain contexts. The question became more one of how to keep Impatience and its negative effects to a minimum and what an acceptable margin of mistakes was for each of them. The discussion enriched all the staff with several new strategies and knowledges about themselves. Most important, they acknowledged that they would feel comfortable talking to each other about It when they needed support.

Why did John run away, despite the pleas of his staff?

John felt overwhelmed by the endless responsibilities. He also resented having to be everything for everyone all the time, especially when he didn't feel he had much power in the end. He really needed "alone time." He grew up as one of nine children and, as a young person, vowed he would take time whenever he needed it. These lunchtimes provided him with energy and self-reflection, something he really wanted to provide for his staff. He didn't realize the effect on his staff until a veteran teacher kindly mentioned it. Once he realized the implications and the problem stories that were circulating about him, he became quite concerned and even considered resigning. John was invited to try a few things before resorting to resignation. He was first invited to listen quietly while his staff was asked to gently map out the effects of "principal absence" on their feelings, thoughts, behaviors, relationships with students, and sense of community. Efforts had to be made initially to keep the tone respectful and constructive, but everyone eventually found a constructive style of sharing. At another meeting, John was interviewed gently in front of his staff as to his experiences as a principal, examples of a typical day, his intentions, values, and attempts to make the best possible decisions. He genuinely apologized, acknowledging that he hadn't realized how important this was for all of them. Ways to minimize the staff's excessive demands on him were explored. Some ideas around reducing student referrals to the office were collectively discussed, determining, first, a short but specific time when teachers would attempt to minimize their visits to him so that he could concentrate on paperwork and, second, the delegating of certain responsibilities that did not need to be accomplished specifically by him. Staff members were shocked when they realized the degree to which he had been burning out, and they were all willing to explore different ways of being together as a community so they could all perform to their own satisfaction.

Why was Chris so distant with this woman, when
he was so good with colleagues and children?

The yard duty volunteer lived quite near Chris and knew
of his "secret" life. Chris had not revealed his homosexuality
to the staff and was concerned about public opinion, especially in the wake of the very positive attention he currently
received from the staff. Chris had quite a bit of anxiety about
this situation, as he feared being misunderstood and judged
by some families and staff members. Worry that the yard duty
volunteer would spill the beans, as he knew that she knew,
made him avoid her at every possible turn.

The situation was eventually solved indirectly by facilitating a staff discussion externalizing the Pressure to be a good
conservative role model and its implications. As part of this
process, the staff and principal grew interested in further-
ing their awareness of diversity issues. A series of workshops
on cultural awareness and tolerance was facilitated, and it
became visible to all that this staff's intentions were to be
open-minded and accepting of a variety of differences. After
a few conversations on diversity and the effects of the pressure, people became more trustful of their community, and it
became more comfortable for several of them to share a
variety of experiences. Over time Chris worked on his own
personal discomfort and was eventually able to share about
his lifestyle with some staff, which eliminated the problematic
secrecy.

Resource A

Glossary

Audience   A group of people that witness a protagonist in a certain way. Since we see ourselves through others' eyes, audiences can be very important in supporting our preferred view of ourselves. In other words, if people see us as clever, it will be easier to experience ourselves as clever. For example: Groups of people such as families, classrooms, and communities who witness our different ways of being.

Contextual blocks   Invisible pressures that limit people's sense of possible ways of being. Originally connected to a culture's set of discourses and specifications, these pressures intersect in complex and unique ways for each individual. Contextual blocks prevent individuals from conceiving of certain options. For example: Pressures such as overdoing, overcontrolling, or being responsible at all costs.

Discourse   A pervasive and insidious cultural system of beliefs and customs that shapes people's lives at all levels (i.e., language, thoughts, feelings, behaviors, dreams, values, expectations, roles, relationships, understandings, lifestyle, politics, etc.). Discourses provide guidelines and assumptions that direct the manner in which people experience their lives. Discourses structure so much of individuals' lives that it is rare to question them and impossible to completely escape them. One can only learn to become aware of their effects and make choices as to which prescriptions may be more congruent with preferred ways of being. For example: individualism, capitalism, and so forth.

Externalization   The process of acknowledging that people's identities are separate from unwanted problems. Problems are treated as entities external to one's sense of self because they are believed to develop as a result of complex and unique experiences of contextual blocks (originating from discourses). For example: I wonder if overworking gets in the way of having friends.

Problem   An unhelpful way of being that can be named, explored, circumvented, and clearly distinguished from an individual's preferred identity. Problems usually develop when people are unable to successfully fulfill the pressures in the contexts of their lives (specifications of a particular discourse); or if they attempt to fulfill the pressures but feel unhappy with the results. For example: "Yelling habits," "Self-doubt," "Worries," to name some.

Preferred story   A series of experiences that becomes articulated as representing one's preferred way of being. For a story to become salient in one's life, it must be connected to relationships, witnessed by an audience, and explored across time. For example: People now think of me as a Helpful person.

Problem story   A problematic way of being that has come to be taken as a representation of an individual's identity. Problem stories can often take over people's lives in such a way that their actual values, special talents, and successes in avoiding the problem become discounted or unnoticed. For example: "Everyone thinks I'm strict, and I really hate that reputation."

Specification   A cultural pressure that prescribes very specific ways of being and that originates from cultural discourses. It is usually identifiable by its implication that an individual "should" or "shouldn't" engage in a certain behavior. For example: Principals should not be too sensitive.

Unique outcome An action or event that illustrates a person's preferred identity and that could not have been predicted given a problem story. For example: Seeing a teacher with a problem reputation for being mean engaging in devoted tutoring for a struggling student.

Resource B

Staff Development Activities

Merging Stories Exercise

Participants co-construct a single story of their lives as if they were one person. Through this process, they notice how rich and diverse each person's experience has been, how their stories do not encompass all of their lived experience, how we naturally narrate our lives as stories, and how stories are co-constructed in relationships and interactions.

Goals

- To notice to what extent people's lives are shaped differently by their sociocultural environments
- To makes visible the process of experiencing our lives as stories
- To notice how being in a relationship involves coauthoring a joint story—to deepen intimacy and connectedness by allowing participants to share historically salient events in their lives

Group Size

Unlimited

Time

30–45 minutes

SOURCE: From *Working With Groups to Enhance Relations,* by Marie-Nathalie Beaudoin and Sue Walden. Copyright 1998 by Whole Person Associates. Reprinted with permission of Whole Person Associates.

Materials

None

Process

1. Ask participants to pair with a partner with whom they feel comfortable sharing aspects of their life experience.

2. Provide the following introduction:

    • We all typically have a story of our lives based on certain salient events or experience that are tied together in a linear sequence. Our lived experience is much richer than this story we tell. How do we determine which events we include in our story and which ones we don't? Events that we remember and include in our narrative are typically the ones that have involved interaction with others and a certain meaning. In that sense we can say that our stories of ourselves are co-constructed.

    • In this exercise, you will be invited to co-construct a story by merging aspects of each of your lives into one single story.

    • Through this process, I would also like to invite you to notice how differently you have been shaped by your social environment. If it feels comfortable and it occurs to you, feel free to include a statement about the social discourses or the contextual constraints that affected that particular experience.

    • Concretely, this means that one person will start by making a *short one- or two-sentence* statement about his or her birth, then the other person will make one or two statements about an event in his or her first year of life, then the first person will continue with a statement about his or her second year, and so on. This alternating process would give a listener the impression that it is one person telling the story.

3. It is often helpful to give an example with your cofacilitator.

For example:

- *Participant 1:* When I was born my mother was so shamed by her religious community that she had to place me for adoption;
- *Participant 2:* When I was one year old my parents moved to San Francisco because my father's job was relocated;
- *Participant 1:* When I was two years old I fell on the floor, broke my leg, and we couldn't afford the surgery I needed to fully recover.

4. Remind participants to make only one or two statements as the game is already quite long, and people typically enjoy it so much that they easily elaborate on each event.

5. When half of the group is done, instruct the others to wrap up within the next five minutes, and ask the ones who are done to discuss their experience of the exchange.

6. Conclude with a discussion of their experience and of the following questions:
   - What was it like to coauthor a single story?
   - What did you notice about your own storying process?
   - Where you surprised by the level of differences and similarities in your lives?
   - Did you become aware of any privileges you may have had that your partner didn't have?
   - How are your behaviors, emotions, and thoughts affected by the stories you tell of yourself?
   - How can that knowledge of your mutual stories affect your relationships?
   - (With couples) Are you now understanding aspects of your partner's life that were confusing to you before?

Post-it Puzzle

This activity offers a powerful way to experientially discover each person's strategies to communicate in an effective and efficient way.

Goal

- To invite participants to notice their ideas and strategies on how to send clear messages
- To increase participants' awareness of the effect of their way of communicating

Group Size

Unlimited number of pairs

Time

30–45 minutes

Materials

Rectangular paper (6" × 9") with the picture of an arrangement of eight to ten Post-its (any arrangement of Post-its can work; readers wishing an example can consult Beaudoin & Walden, 1997), and cardboard (6" × 9") with movable shaped Post-its. One of each of the pairs needs the picture, and the partner needs the cardboard.

Process

1. Invite participants to sit back-to-back with their partners along a straight line with about three feet between them and other pairs on either side of them (if space allows).

2. Introduce the activity by telling the participants:
   - This game involves communicating a set of instructions in a limited amount of time

- Participants will use only verbal communication to complete the task and are not to look over each other's shoulders

3. Show the partners who will have the picture an example of the cardboard and movable Post-its; then show the partner who will have the cardboard an example (not the real one, of course) of a picture that their partner will be working with.

4. Hand out the picture of the arrangement of triangles to all the partners facing one way and the cardboard with the Post-it triangles to their partners sitting behind them.

5. Participants with the picture must communicate clear instructions to their partners on how to reproduce what they see by arranging the Post-it triangles. Both participants need to clarify and verify their understanding of the information both sent and received.

6. Signal to start, allowing three to five minutes to complete the task.

7. After calling time, allow a few minutes for the partners to compare the original picture and the Post-it picture and discuss their process.

8. Roles are changed and new pictures are supplied.

9. Conclude the exercise by asking participants to discuss some of the following questions:
   - What worked and what didn't work in achieving this task?
   - What strategies did you discover to facilitate the process?
   - What caused miscommunication?
   - Did certain words have different meanings for each of you? Can you share examples?
   - How is this exercise similar to and/or different from your day-to-day communications?

Resource C

Summary of School Culture Problems and the Practices That Prevent Them

Externalized Problems (from Chapter 3)	Remedies (from Chapter 6)	Examples of Positive Practices
Gossip	Connection Appreciation Leadership	• Provide more visibility of educators' private lives • Embrace a genuine philosophy of valuing differences • Create a context for communication and a space where problem solving occurs (forums, e-mails, meetings, honest conversations) • Share appreciation for others • Redefine leadership as a difference of role • Share a democratic process for change and make intentions and constraints visible for unpopular decisions • Have a commitment to team building • Host a community discussion on the effects of the gossip habit
Problem-saturated communication	Appreciation Self-reflection	• Remember the effects and implications of problem-saturated communication • Have a general agreement not to speak negatively in the staff room

Externalized Problems (from Chapter 3)	Remedies (from Chapter 6)	Examples of Positive Practices
		• Structure events that make appreciation visible between educators, students, and parents (e.g., singing telegrams, letter day) • Use self-reflection as a way to unwind
Cliques	Appreciation Collaboration	• Start staff meetings with appreciations • Facilitate retreats where each person's educational values are visible • Host workshops on valuing diversity, strengthening the importance of belonging to a community • Hold fun staff events • Promote vertical and horizontal collaboration • Keep your staff seating arrangement in mind
The Us-Them attitude	Connection Collaboration Leadership	• Connect with your staff • Create a spirit of collaboration • Minimize hierarchy and embrace reciprocal leadership • Develop relationships with union representatives • Make your intentions visible • Hire an ombudsperson to facilitate meetings
Resentment and negativity	Appreciation Connection Self-reflection	• Host an individual compassionate meeting with an educator struggling with a critical problem story • Review the pressures of the specifications • Study the feasibility of meeting the demands made on staff members • Share appreciation; this is essential in rendering the profession more rewarding and satisfying

Externalized Problems (from Chapter 3)	Remedies (from Chapter 6)	Examples of Positive Practices
		• Keep staff engaged in staff development, creating a context that inspires curious learners of all ages (examples include: invite speakers, read books, attend professional development courses, reflect upon goals/values)
Community disrespect	Connection Collaboration	• Involve parents and grandparents in many roles on campus • Create a space for teachers to be seen as people with unique talents (not just as "teacher") • Make teachers' work visible (newsletter acknowledging each teacher's biography/ programs) • Contact the media about positive events (if reporters have relationships with the schools, they are less likely to bash) • Work on community service projects • Involve local businesses by their adopting a school and sending in volunteers • Reevaluate your vision of self as an educator as well as the nature of relationships you want to have with staff, students, and community
Rushed feeling/Scarcity of time	Self-Reflection Collaboration Appreciation	• Discuss how the pressures to perform affect the unique community and the staff • Facilitate staff conversation to clarify their priorities as a group • Make time for self-reflection, articulating and holding onto what energizes you as an educator

Externalized Problems (from Chapter 3)	Remedies (from Chapter 6)	Examples of Positive Practices
		• Involve community members to assist with demands • Collaborate on planning, chores, etc.
Hierarchy	Collaboration Leadership Connection	• Introduce cross-age buddies who meet weekly, between teachers (a teacher can befriend a kid from another class and age group) • Facilitate groups of administrators, teachers, parents, and students to meet, study, and debate issues • Promote vertical collaboration between grade-level teams • Create a context where everyone can be at their best • Connect with people as people; be accessible, visible, open, and inclusive • Encourage a more democratic environment
Competition	Collaboration Appreciation Connection	• Collaborate on many levels • Share appreciation for self and others • Facilitate a staff conversation about the sneaky habit of competition • Find alternative ways to promote enthusiasm • Have individuals set their own goals for performance and be self-reflective on their own progress • Reward all for efforts (e.g., gift certificates for educators or joint celebration for classes) • Create a context where everyone can be at their best

Resource D

Job Satisfaction Survey

As discussed elsewhere in this book, we have interviewed and/or surveyed well over 200 educators from a wide range of elementary and middle public schools, mostly in North California. The populations in these schools varied in terms of socioeconomic status, race, and ethnicity. Schools were visited in rural and suburban areas as well as in the city. Four schools involved parent participation; the remaining were general public schools. Here are some of the survey and interview questions that we have used. As we progressed in the research, some questions were eliminated, some improved, and some were added or modified to suit the particular school staff we were visiting. These are provided here as examples of possible surveys that can be helpful to use in your own school.

BRIEF JOB SATISFACTION SURVEY

Please answer ALL questions.
Thank you for your time!

Gender: M   F

Years of teaching experience: _____

Please circle your choice.

How would you rate your overall job satisfaction?

1. Lacking   2. Tolerable   3. Acceptable   4. Good   5. Excellent

What are the three most important contributors to your job satisfaction?

_____

_____

_____

How would you generally characterize your relationship with your teaching colleagues?

1. Lacking   2. Tolerable   3. Acceptable   4. Good   5. Excellent

Would you like to be more connected with your colleagues?

Yes   No   Okay as is

How: _____

Is your educational philosophy similar to that of the majority of the staff?

Yes   No

Specifically, _____

Do you feel that overall the staff is homogeneous in terms of educational philosophy?

Yes   No

At school, how many teachers would you trust with personal information? _____

Are the teachers at your school willing to share material and collaborate with you?

1. Never   2. Occasionally   3. Sometimes   4. Most of the time   5. Always

Do you feel appreciated by the rest of the staff?

1. Never   2. Occasionally   3. Sometimes   4. Most of the time   5. Always

How would you generally characterize your relationship with your principal?

1. Lacking   2. Tolerable   3. Acceptable   4. Good   5. Excellent

Would you like to be more connected with your principal?

Yes   No   Okay as is

How: _____

How much do you appreciate the leadership style of your principal?

1. Not at all   2. Sometimes   3. Generally   4. Mostly   5. Very much

Any suggestions: _____

Please circle only what characterizes the leadership style of your principal and its extent (1. A little   2. Sometimes 3. Very much)

Trusting	*Appreciative*	*Democratic in Most Decisions*	*Approachable*
1 2 3	1 2 3	1 2 3	1 2 3

Micro-Manages	*Evaluates*	*Unilateral Decision Making*	*Distant*
1 2 3	1 2 3	1 2 3	1 2 3

How connected do you feel to most of your students?

1. Not at all   2. Somewhat   3. Generally   4. Mostly   5. Very

What percentage of the time do you experience disrespect from students? _____

Do you like to have parents assist you in the classroom?

1. Not at all   2. Maybe   3. Not sure   4. Probably   5. Very much

Do you currently benefit from parent assistance in the classroom?

1. Not at all   2. Somewhat   3. Generally   4. Most of the time   5. Very much

If you were to write a creative or powerful statement/ metaphor about what it is like to be a teacher, what would it be?

_____

_____

_____

Resource E

Teacher Survey

We are writing a book on bullying and other school culture issues. We really appreciate your input. These surveys are confidential, and you may choose to remain anonymous.

Years of experience (including this year): _____

Gender: M   F

How often do you experience the following? Please circle a number.

The pressure to be a good role model

1. Never   2. Rarely   3. Sometimes   4. Half of   5. Most of   6. Always
                                          the time   the time

Please define what you personally mean by "good role model."

The need to be a dedicated teacher

1. Never   2. Rarely   3. Sometimes   4. Half of   5. Most of   6. Always
                                          the time   the time

Having to sacrifice personal time to get the job done

1. Never   2. Rarely   3. Sometimes   4. Half of   5. Most of   6. Always
                                          the time   the time

The pressure to be organized and well prepared (beyond your personal standards)

1. Never   2. Rarely   3. Sometimes   4. Half of   5. Most of   6. Always
                                          the time   the time

The pressure to know all the answers all the time with:

Your colleagues

1. Never   2. Rarely   3. Sometimes   4. Half of   5. Most of   6. Always
                                          the time   the time

Your students

1. Never   2. Rarely   3. Sometimes   4. Half of   5. Most of   6. Always
                                          the time   the time

Your students' parents

1. Never   2. Rarely   3. Sometimes   4. Half of   5. Most of   6. Always
                                          the time   the time

The need to be in control of your students (beyond your personal preference)

1. Never   2. Rarely   3. Sometimes   4. Half of   5. Most of   6. Always
                                          the time   the time

How do you define being in control?

Does standardized testing fit in your educational philosophy? Please explain.

How does the pressure for good test scores affect you as a teacher?

How does the pressure for good test scores affect your relationship with your students?

What percentage of the time do you enjoy your job as a teacher? _____. Please give an example.

Things principals in general may do that are positive, helpful, and supportive:

Things principals in general may do that are negative, upsetting, or instill self-doubt:

Things other teachers do that are positive, helpful, and supportive:

Things other teachers may do that are negative, upsetting, or instill self-doubt:

Resource F

Principal Interview Protocol

REWARDS

What are your biggest rewards?

What do your students see in you that they appreciate?

What do you think is the most important thing a kid gets out of a relationship with the principal?

What do you think is the most important thing a kid gets out of time at your school?

Remember a student who made a profound impact on you.

What do your staff members see in you that they appreciate?

Is there a teacher you worked with that had a profound affect on you? What was it?

Is there a parent from whom you really learned something?

CHALLENGES

What is your biggest struggle?

Was there a child you felt that your school couldn't help?

How does competition affect you and your staff (between teachers, between schools, for test scores, etc.)?

How do you handle the pressures from the district office and the state?

What philosophy do you have when dealing with parents who have a conflict with a teacher?

How do you deal with union issues?

What is the effect of the union on your job?

How do you deal with having to choose a teacher—without favoritism—for a position (master teacher, committee member, curriculum specialist, vice-principal) if teachers from your staff are vying for the same position?

How do you deal with a teacher who doesn't want to do anything new and wants to stick closely to the contract?

How do you deal with a teacher who has a negative attitude?

How do you deal with a staff that is in an "us-them" relationship with you and the district administration?

What do you keep in mind when you are trying to communicate with a staff member?

Ideal School

How do you promote bonding with your staff?

How do you promote collaboration among teachers and between teachers and yourself?

How do you express appreciation for individual staff members without creating favoritism?

How do you reduce the effects of isolation?

How do you reduce the effects of evaluation on you and your staff (from parents, the district administration, and the public)?

SPECIFICATION STORIES

Do you feel that principals are expected to know everything about everything? Why do you think this is? What are the effects of this?

Some principals have told us that they felt like they needed to serve everyone's needs at all times. Do you feel that this is true? Is there an example that comes to your mind?

Other principals have told us that they feel pressure to be in control of their teachers. This pressure seems to come from society and parents. Is that a part of your experience as well?

Principals have also expressed that they feel responsible for being political and being the school visionary. Do you feel pressure to create the vision for your school and inspire the community? What does this look like when you are doing this?

A PRINCIPAL'S LIFE

What would you like parents to know?

What do you wish teachers understood about your work?

If you were to come up with a metaphor about being a principal, what would it be?

What is the difference between your dreams and expectations of your job and the realities of the job?

What would you change if you could?

Do you have a dream for yourself professionally? Personally?

References

Ashton-Jones, E., Olson G. A., & Perry, M. G. (2000). *The gender reader.* Needham Heights, MA: A. Pearson Education Company.

Beaudoin, M.-N., & Taylor, M. (2004). *Breaking the culture of bullying and disrespect, grades K-8.* Thousand Oaks, CA: Corwin Press.

Beaudoin, M.-N., & Walden, S. (1997). *Working with groups to enhance relationships.* Duluth, MN: Whole Person Associates.

Bird, J. (2000). *The heart's narrative.* Auckland, New Zealand: Edge Press.

Bolman, L. G., & Deal, T. E. (2001). *Leading with soul: An uncommon journey of spirit* (rev. ed.). Indianapolis, IN: Jossey-Bass.

Communication Research Associates. (1995). *Communicate: A workbook for interpersonal communication* (5th ed.). Dubuque, IA: Kendall/Hunt.

Education Writers Association. (2002). *Special report on principals.* Available online at www.ewa.org

Freeman, J., & Combs, G. (1996). *Narrative therapy.* New York: Norton.

Freeman, J., Epston, D., & Lobovits, D. (1997). *Playful approaches to serious problems.* New York: Norton.

Gergen, K. (1985). The social constructionist movement in modern psychology. *American Psychologist, 40,* 266–275.

Gergen, K. (1991). *The saturated self: Dilemmas of identity in contemporary life.* New York: Basic Books.

Heatherington, C. (1995). *Celebrating diversity: Working with groups in the workplace.* Duluth, MN: Whole Person Associates.

Hoffman, L. (1990). Constructing realities: An art of lenses. *Family Process, 29,* 1–12.

Johnson Fenner, P. (1995). *Waldorf Education: A family guide.* Amesbury, MA: Michaelmas Press.

Kimmel, M. S., & Messner, M. A. (1998). *Men's lives.* Needham Heights, MA: Allyn & Bacon.

Madsen, W. C. (1999). *Collaborative therapy with multi-stressed families.* New York: Guilford.

Marzano, R. J., & Kendall, J. S. (1998). *Awash in a sea of standards.* Aurora, CO: Mid-continent Research for Education and Learning. (Available online at www.McREL.org)

Merrow, J. (2001). *Choosing excellence.* Lanham, MD: Scarecrow Press.

O'Neil, J. (1995). On schools as learning organizations: A conversation with Peter Senge. *Education Leadership, 52*(7), 20–23.

Pollack, W. (1999). *Real boys.* New York: Henry Holt.

Reiman, J. (2000). *Thinking for a living.* Marietta, GA: Longstreet Press.

Tannen, D. (1990). *You just don't understand.* New York: Ballantine.

White, M., & Epston, D. (1990). *Narrative means to therapeutic ends.* New York: Norton.

Winslade, J., & Monk, G. (1999). *Narrative counseling in schools.* Thousands Oaks, CA: Corwin Press.

Winslade, J., & Monk, G. (2000). *Narrative mediation.* San Francisco: Jossey-Bass.

Zimmerman, J., & Dickerson, V. (1996). *If problems talked.* New York: Guilford.

Index